Woman's Day

Creative Stitchery From Scraps

Edited by Nancy Schraffenberger

Robert J. Kasbar:
Book Coordinator/Production Manager

Designed by *Allan Mogel Studios*

Columbia House, New York

PHOTOGRAPHY CREDITS

Ben Calvo, *Woman's Day* Studio.
All photographs, except as follows:
Carmen Schiavone, pages 13, 19,
  24, 27, 31, 51, 57, 75, 99, 121, 130, 135, 137
Leif Schiller, pages 8, 40
John Stember, pages 109, 150
Ben Marra, page 78
Keith Scott Morton, page 152

DESIGNER CREDITS

Lorraine Bodger, page 106
Audrey Brown, pages 144, 152
Bob Brown, page 118
Gloria Buchwald, page 135
Anita Deming, page 42
Claudia Ein, pages 57, 75, 146
Jan Eisenman, page 99
Laurel Hobbs, page 112
Madge Huntington, page 45
Carol Inouye, page 48
Elizabeth Jaeger, page 34
Pat Jones, page 137
Ruth Katz, pages 24, 51
Ann Kirchner, page 78
Jerry Kott, pages 8, 40
Hilde Liu, pages 60, 130
Joan McElroy, page 13
Patricia C. Miller, page 142
Jennifer Mills, pages 37, 55
Barbara Muccio, pages 10, 127
Joy Nagy, page 102
Pamela Negron, page 124
Martin M. Pegler, page 27
Michiko Sato, page 154
Elizabeth Sayles, page 19
Lia Shepherd, page 115
Roberta Sickler, page 31
Ursula Von Wartburg, page 121
Marilyn Wein, pages 63, 66, 69, 140
Woman's Day Staff, pages 72, 109, 133, 148, 150

Copyright © 1980 CBS Publications, the Consumer
Publishing Division of CBS Inc.

ISBN: 0-930748-16-6
Printed in the United States of America
Published by Columbia House, a Division of CBS Inc.,
1211 Avenue of the Americas, New York, New York 10036

CONTENTS

INTRODUCTION

Anyone who collects bits and pieces of fabric that are just too good to throw away has a small fortune at hand—and a short browse through this collection of boutique designs from the pages of *Woman's Day* will prove it.

For the first time we've gathered together in book form, toys, gifts, and accessories for your home and wardrobe that you can stitch with a scrap of this and a hank of that—or perhaps a sale remnant you picked up to use when exactly the right project came along.

Our scrap designs include slippers and hat trims, animals and aprons, place mats and pillows. Most of the designs require less than a yard of fabric to complete, although we have included a few larger projects (such as a rug and a patchwork spread) that call for a fairly substantial quantity of scrap material.

By no means must you duplicate the prints, colors, or even the fabrics we chose, except in a few cases where a certain weight is recommended or a special texture is desirable. Part of your enjoyment will be deciding that your stuffed reindeer will be striped, your dog coat will be plaid, or your appliquéd pillow will be velvet. The point is, almost any precious remnant you discover—be it satin, felt, pretend-fur, or hopsacking—can be turned into a charming, handmade treasure.

As you expect from *Woman's Day,* the directions for each project are explicit and easy to follow. A special bonus: more than a dozen patterns are full size and all are shown in extra-large scale to make transferring them as simple as possible.

In short, our group of designs represents light and delightful projects and it includes many that are perfect for a grownup and a child to enjoy creating together.

GENERAL INFORMATION

Before you start a sewing project from this book, read the simple guidelines below.

How to Use Full-size Patterns Some of the patterns in this book are actual size. To use them, place a piece of tracing paper or clear vinyl over the book page and trace the outlines of the patterns you will need. Label each piece and cut along outer edges.

How to Enlarge Patterns You will need brown wrapping paper (pieced if necessary to make a sheet large enough for a pattern), a felt-tipped marker, pencil, and ruler. (**Note:** If the pattern you are enlarging has a grid around it, first connect lines across pattern with a colored pencil to form a grid over the picture.) Mark paper with grid as follows: First cut paper into a true square or rectangle. Then mark dots around edges, 1″ or 2″ apart or whatever is indicated on pattern, making the same number of spaces as there are squares around the edges of pattern diagram. Form a grid by joining the dots across opposite sides of paper. Make sure you have the same number of squares as shown in diagram. With a marker, draw in each square the same pattern lines you see in corresponding squares on diagram.

If you don't want to draw a grid to enlarge your pattern, you can order a package of four 22″ x 34″ sheets of 1″ graph paper for $2 postpaid, from Sewmakers, Inc., 1623 Grand Ave., Baldwin, N.Y. 11510.

How to Cut Patterns From Fabric Plan the placement of the patterns on the wrong side of the fabric you are using, being sure to allow 1″ between the pieces for seams. If two pieces of the same pattern piece are to be cut, reverse the pattern to cut the second

6

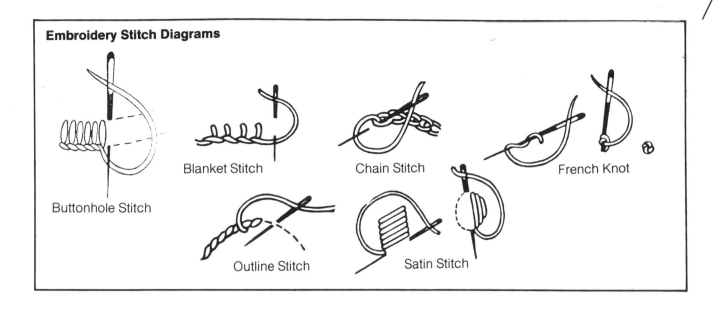

Embroidery Stitch Diagrams

Buttonhole Stitch

Blanket Stitch

Chain Stitch

French Knot

Outline Stitch

Satin Stitch

piece. If the fabric has a nap, as does velveteen, be sure to place all pattern pieces so that the nap runs in the same direction. Pin each pattern in place. With a soft pencil, outline each pattern on the fabric. This outline will be your *stitching guideline.* Cut out the pattern pieces, *adding whatever seam allowance, if any, is specified.*

How to Stitch Items to Be Stuffed Machine-stitch, using a fine (size 11) needle to keep the needle holes small. Double-stitch the seams around stuffing openings to reinforce them.

After sewing each seam, check for "jogs" or loose stitches and restitch if necessary. All uncorrected bumps and jogs will show after you turn and stuff the item. Trim the seam allowance to ¼" and clip V notches into it on curved edges.

Turn pieces carefully to the right side. Tiny pieces may need gentle encouragement with a long, blunt crochet hook or knitting needle to turn completely.

How to Stuff Polyester fiberfill is preferred for stuffing because it is smooth, resilient, and washable. Kapok and cotton batting can be used for items that won't be washed if you are careful to pull apart and soften any lumps in the filling when you stuff.

Fold masking tape over the raw cloth edges of openings to reduce fraying and to hold the edges open when you insert the stuffing. Insert *small* bits of stuffing and push them gently into the corners with a blunt crochet hook. Stuff until item is firm and smooth. Remove the tape and sew closed using a blindstitch. Continue to add stuffing as you sew the openings closed, in order to keep the sewn area as firm as the rest of the item.

Hearts and Flowers "Jewelry"

Plump little hearts, each holding a miniature bouquet, make engaging fashion accents. The bracelet is a stuffed tube of satin; the large and small pendants are suspended on rattail. We used shiny polka-dot satin for the hearts, but they'd be equally charming in any small-figure print.

MATERIALS: ⅛ yard 36″-wide polka-dot red satin; 2¼″ x 8½″ piece of plain red satin and 8½″ length of ½″-diameter welting cord for bracelet; red sewing thread; bunch of tiny white artificial flowers; ¾ yard heavy white rattail (satin cord) for each pendant; bits of absorbent cotton.

BRACELET: Transfer pattern for bracelet to tracing paper and cut out 3 full hearts from polka-dot satin, adding ¼″ to all edges for seam allowance. Fold to wrong side a lobe of 1 heart along broken line; place folded heart, right side up, on right side of another heart and baste hearts together. (Folded section forms pocket.) With right sides facing, stitch assembled heart to remaining single heart, leaving opening for turning. Clip seam allowance along curves, turn heart; pad firmly. Sew opening closed. Tack flowers in pocket.

Fold plain satin strip in half lengthwise, wrong side out. Making ¼″ seam, stitch long edge to form tube. Turn; insert welting cord in tube. Fold in ends of tube and sew them to back of heart.

PENDANTS: Transfer pattern for 1 or both pendants to tracing paper and cut out. Cut out, assemble, and stuff heart as for bracelet. Tack flowers in pocket.

Tie knot in center of cord; tack knot between lobes of heart. Knot each end of cord.

Full-size Patterns for Hearts and Flowers "Jewelry"

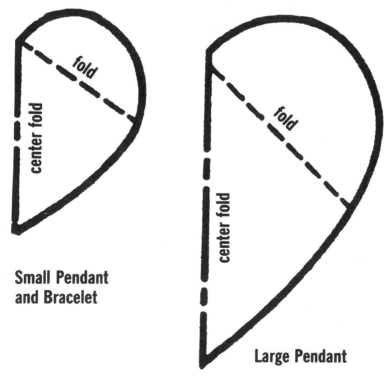

Small Pendant and Bracelet

Large Pendant

SLEEPYHEAD APPLIQUÉD PILLOWS

The sweetly dreaming elf and bonneted baby sleep on small pillows that could be endearing wall accents for a child's room—which is why they're made with loops for hanging. All you need are bits and pieces of lace, ribbon, and fabric—the faces are drawn with felt-tip markers.

ELF PILLOW

SIZE: 7½'' x 10''.

MATERIALS: One 8½'' by 11'' piece each of 2 different cotton prints (1 print should be red and white); scrap of fuzzy red fabric for elf suit; scrap of flesh-colored felt for face; 16'' strip of ½''-wide white cotton lace; matching sewing thread; 3 lace flowers; white or fabric glue; 2'' scrap of white ribbon to hang pillow; fine-tipped felt marker, polyester-fiberfill stuffing.

Transfer elf pattern to tracing paper and cut out. Cut full elf suit from fuzzy fabric (do not add seam allowance). Cut out hole for face. Loop lace across suit and under arms (see broken line on pattern).

Full-size Pattern for Sleepyhead Appliquéd Pillow (Elf)

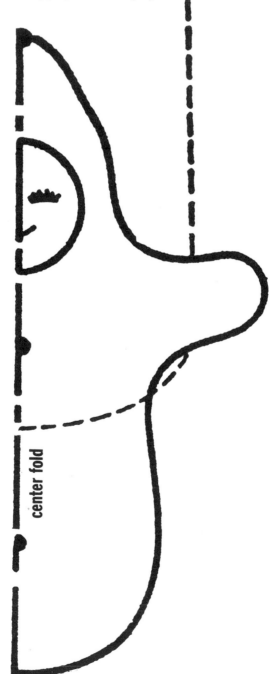

center fold

Machine-appliqué suit to center of red-and white print, using close zigzag stitch. Topstitch lace in place.

From flesh-colored felt, cut circle face to fit opening in suit; glue in place. Draw smiling eyes and mouth with marker. Tack 3 lace flowers to suit.

With right sides facing, stitch pillow front and back together with ½" seams, leaving top edge open. Turn and stuff. Sew opening closed, catching ends of 2" ribbon scrap for hanging loop.

BABY PILLOW

SIZE: 9½" x 10½".

MATERIALS: Two 10½" x 11½" pieces of cotton print; 4½" x 6½" piece of red flannel; 2½" x 3½" piece of white cotton fabric; scrap of flesh-colored felt for face; matching sewing thread; white or fabric glue; 21" strip of 1"-wide lace; 16" strip of ½"-wide white cotton lace; 2 tiny cotton lace flowers; 22" strip of ¼"-wide white satin ribbon; fine-tipped felt marker; polyester-fiberfill stuffing.

Following photograph for placement, pin white fabric for baby pillow to a piece of print fabric. Pin narrow lace along top and 2 sides of white pillow, red flannel for blanket, wide lace along top and 2 sides of blanket. Cut 1½"-diameter felt circle for face; glue to pillow. With marker draw sleeping eyes and smiling mouth. Touch cheeks with pink pencil, rouge, or lipstick. Sew gathered narrow lace around face.

Stitch border of ribbon along top and sides of white pillow; tie 2 tiny ribbon bows and tack 1 at each corner of ribbon band. Tack a lace flower above each bow. Make long-streamered ribbon bow and sew to blanket.

With right sides facing, stitch pillow front and back together with ½" seams, leaving top edge open. Turn and stuff. Sew opening closed, catching ends of 2" ribbon scrap for hanging loop.

Hand-Puppet Family

Mama, papa, sister, and brother are represented in this theatrical family of hand puppets. The materials are scraps of felt and bulky gift-tie yarn. Details of puppets' clothing and their facial features are glued on.

Instructions on following pages ➤

HAND-PUPPET FAMILY

MATERIALS: Various colors scrap felt; small buttons; jingle bell; various colors scrap yarn, especially the bulky gift-tie yarn for hair; matching sewing thread; white glue.

BOY: Transfer patterns for body, shirt, overalls, and hands to tracing paper and cut out. Using patterns, cut from felt two body pieces, two shirt pieces, two overall pieces (back piece with shoulder straps), and four hand pieces. Following pattern and photograph for placement, center a shirt piece on each body piece; stitch together across neck. Add a hand at end of each shirt sleeve; stitch across wrist. Center front and back overall pieces on assembled body-shirt pieces; stitch top edge the width of neck only. Center assembled front on assembled back, wrong sides together, and whipstitch side edges all around, leaving bottom edges open.

Bring overall shoulder straps to front and tack in place with buttons as shown. Cut two felt squares in contrasting color for overall pockets; glue in place. Cut facial features from felt and glue in place. For hair, cut six or seven short pieces of gift-tie yarn; stitch pieces together across center. Arrange on head and tack in place securely as in photograph.

GIRL: Transfer patterns for body and dress to tracing paper; transfer to felt and cut two body pieces with hands and two dress pieces. Center a dress piece on a body piece as in photograph, and topstitch pieces together across neck and hem edge of dress. Put assembled front and back pieces together and whipstitch around all side edges, leaving bottom open.

From pattern cut out felt flower and cuff bands in contrasting colors. Glue flower to front of dress and cuffs on wrist edge of sleeves. Tack bell to center of flower as in photograph. Cut facial features from felt; glue in place. For hair, cut three lengths of gift-tie yarn long enough to go around head for loose braids. Join lengths across center and tack in place on head. Tie loose bunches of yarn hair with thin yarn as in photograph; tack to sides securely.

Girl

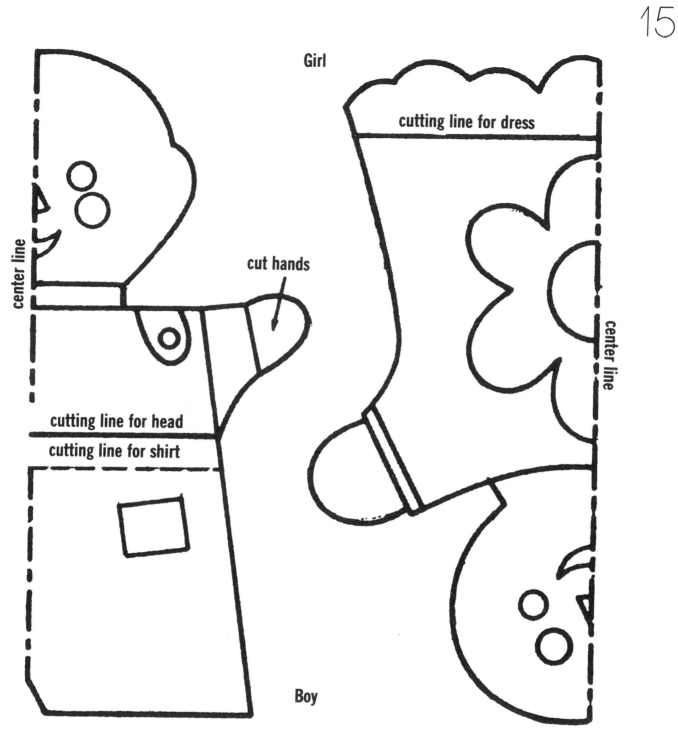

center line

cut hands

cutting line for dress

center line

cutting line for head

cutting line for shirt

Boy

Full-size Patterns for Hand-puppet Family

FATHER: Transfer patterns for head, hands, shirt, vest, and pants to tracing paper; transfer to felt and cut two heads, four hands, two shirts, two pants, and one front and one back vest piece. Stitch head to shirt neck and hands to shirt sleeves. Center vest pieces on shirt and topstitch at armhole and neck edges. Add pants and topstitch bottom edge of vest to join. Center assembled front on back and whipstitch all side edges, leaving bottom open.

Using pattern, cut tie and glue in place. Also cut facial features and glue in place. Trim front of vest with 3 buttons as shown in photograph. For hair, cut 3 or 4 short lengths of gift-tie yarn and stitch across in 3 places. Tack hair to back of head and bring ends to sides of head for fringe.

MOTHER: Transfer patterns for head, hands, dress, and apron to tracing paper; transfer to felt and cut out two heads, four hands, two dress pieces, and apron. Stitch head to dress neck and hands to sleeves. Center apron on one joined head and dress piece; topstitch around neck, side, and bottom edges. Cut a narrow curved strip to go across back neckline of remaining joined head and dress piece for halter of apron; topstitch in place. Center assembled front on back and whipstitch around all side edges, leaving bottom open.

From pattern cut felt flower for apron in contrasting colors; glue in place. Also cut facial features and glue in place. For apron ties cut two lengths of thin yarn; tie in bow. Center bow on back of puppet, bring loose ends around front and tack to sides of apron; clip excess. For hair, coil length of gift-tie yarn into 2"-diameter disk; tack to back of head. Fold another length of yarn around top edge of disk, bring around to front and sides of head, and tack in place securely.

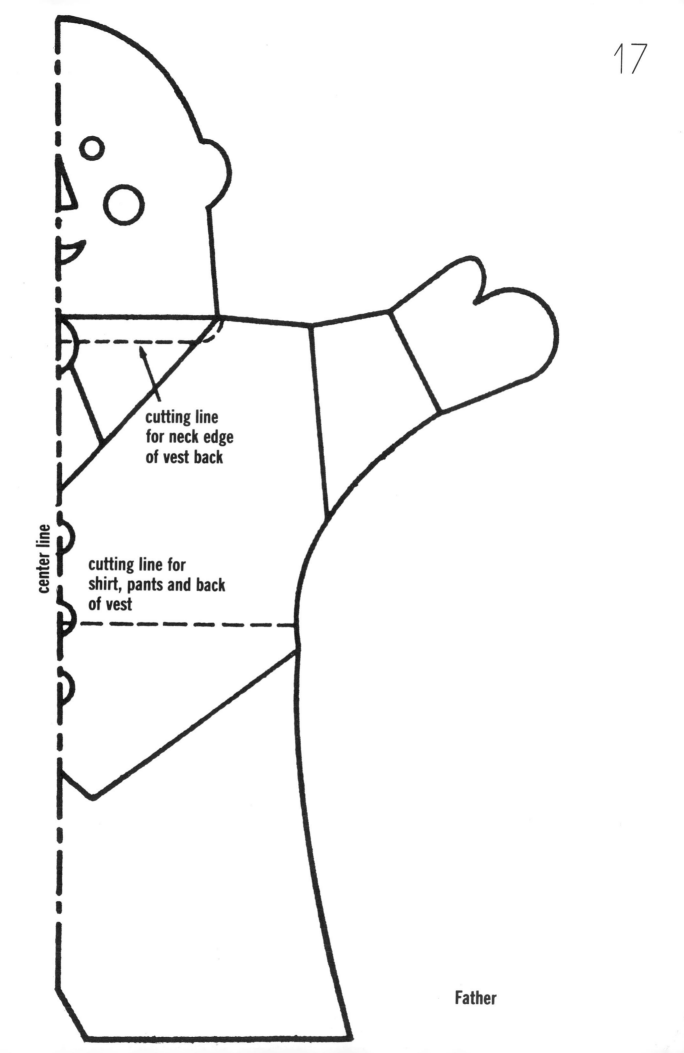

center line

cutting line
for neck edge
of vest back

cutting line for
shirt, pants and back
of vest

Father

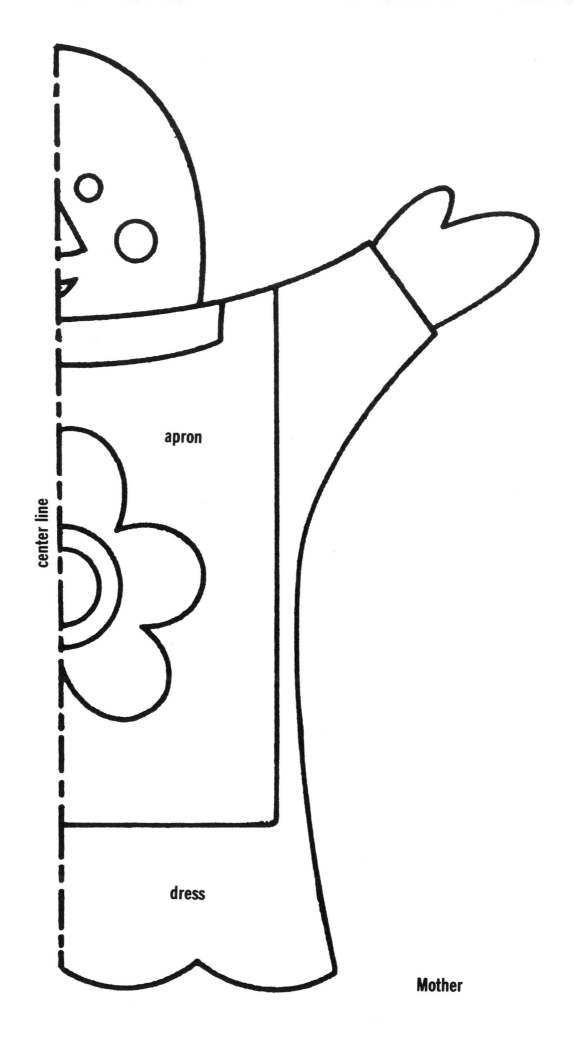

center line

apron

dress

18

Mother

Whimsical Hat Trims

You won't even need a needle and thread for these—just scissors, felt, glue, and a big, plain straw hat. The motifs, cut from felt scraps, are (left to right) a pair of saucy tropical birds streaming ribbony tails; an ocean wave teeming with fish, seaweed, and such; and a hatful of flowers.

Instructions on following pages >

WHIMSICAL HAT TRIMS

TROPICAL BIRDS
MATERIALS: Large-brimmed straw hat; pieces of felt in red, turquoise, gold, white, and black; ½''-wide satin ribbon, 2¼ yards each red, pink, and green, 1¼ yards yellow; white glue.

Transfer patterns for bird, wing and beak to tracing paper. From felt cut 2 red birds, 2 turquoise wings, and 2 gold beaks. For eyes, cut larger circles from white felt and smaller circles from black felt.

Following photograph, pin birds on opposite sides of hat.

For bird tails, cut all ribbons into 20'' lengths. For each tail, overlap ribbons as follows, fanning out colors at one end: 1 red, 1 pink, 1 green, 1 yellow, 1 red, 1 pink and 1 green. Glue ribbons underneath tail end of bird.

Glue birds in place, using pins to hold until dry. Cut free ends of ribbons at an angle. Glue wings and beaks to birds. For eyes, glue black piece over white, then glue to bird.

MARINE SCENE
MATERIALS: Large-brimmed straw hat; pieces of felt in turquoise, 3 shades of green, beige, hot pink, fuchsia, gold, salmon pink, and black; white glue.

Transfer patterns for small fish, large fish, starfish, seaweed, and wave band to tracing paper. From turquoise felt cut wave band, repeating pattern until band is long enough to fit around crown plus 1'' for overlap. From felt cut 2 beige starfish, 4 seaweeds in assorted shades of green, 1 large hot-pink fish, 2 small fuchsia fish and 1 small fish each in gold, salmon, and black. For eyes, cut 4 black felt and 2 turquoise felt circles.

Glue wave band to hat, using pins to hold in place until dry. Following photograph (or as desired), glue fish and seaweed on band and eyes on fish.

BUDS AND BLOSSOMS
MATERIALS: Large-brimmed straw hat; pieces of felt in dark green, medium green, black, beige, orange, coral, and fuchsia; white glue.

Transfer patterns for leaf and flower petals to tracing paper.

Full-size Patterns for Whimsical Hat Trims

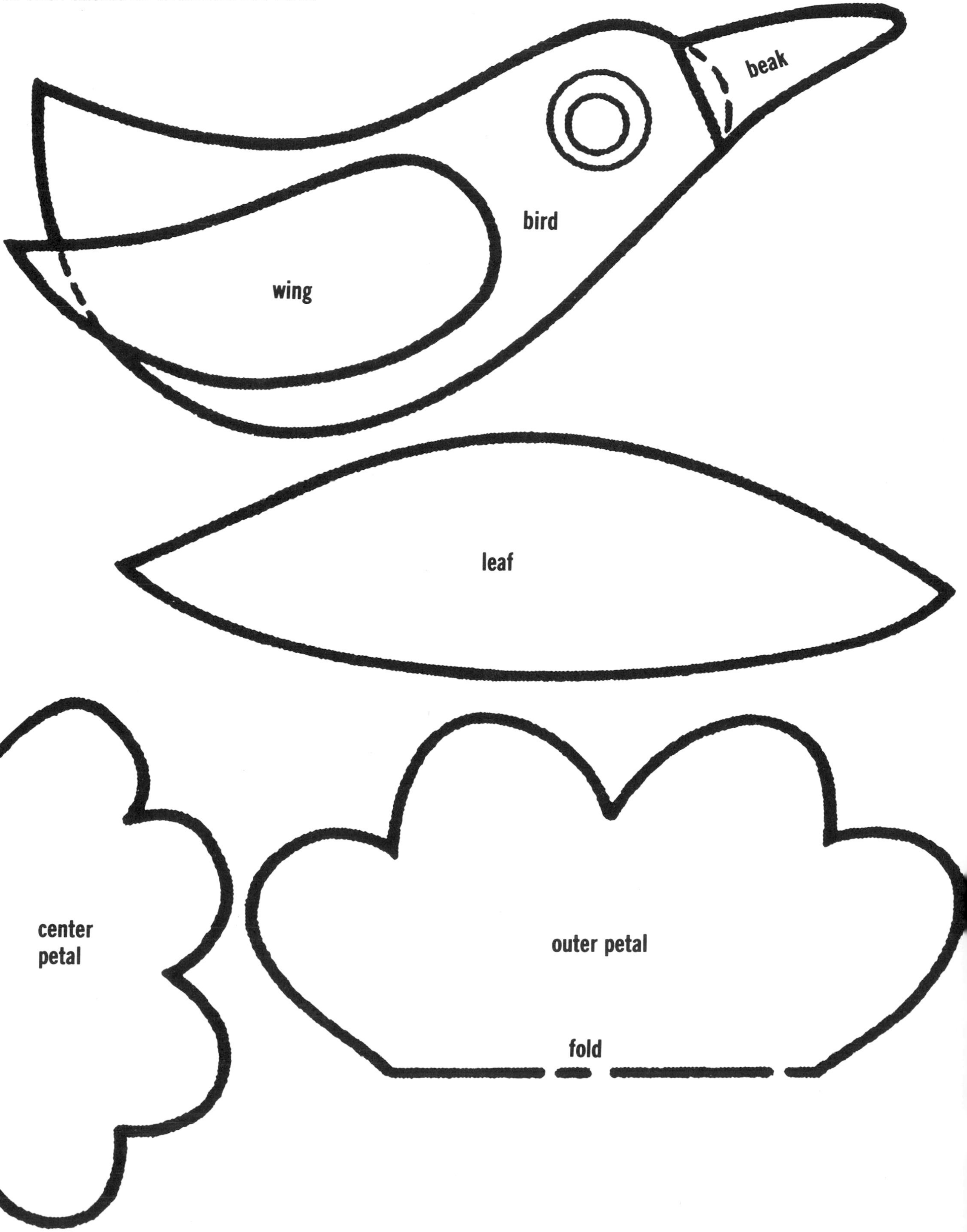

beak

bird

wing

leaf

center petal

outer petal

fold

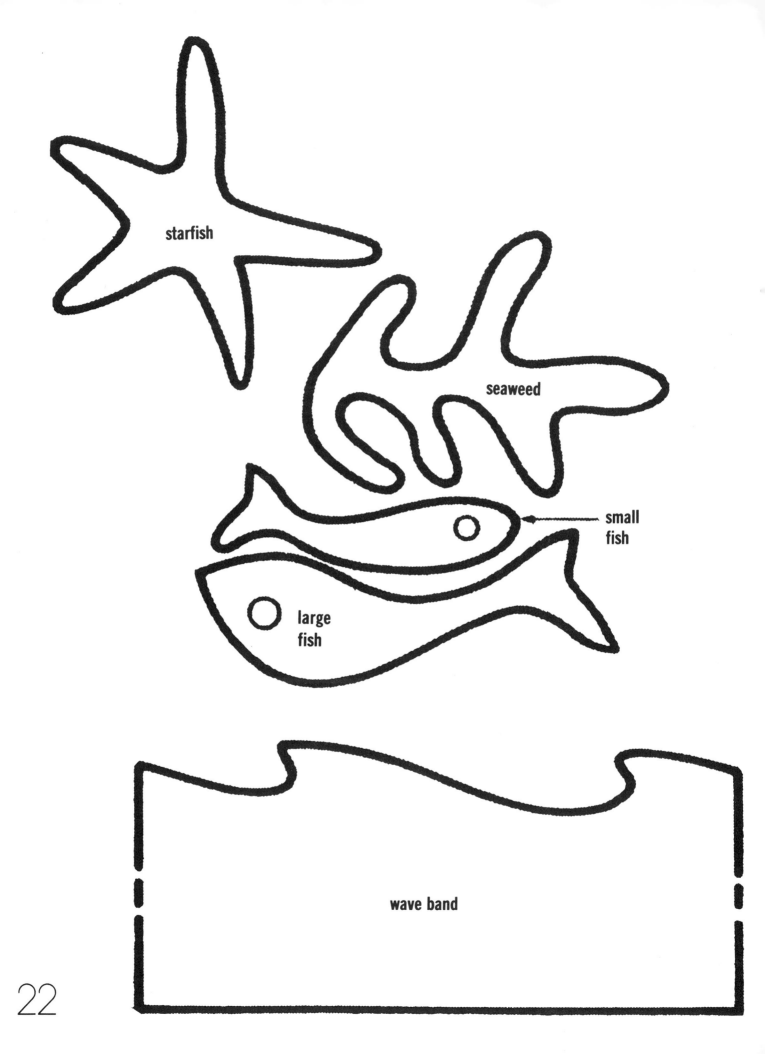

starfish

seaweed

small
fish

large
fish

wave band

22

From felt, using outer petal pattern, cut 2 each orange, coral, fuchsia, and beige. Using center petal pattern, cut 4 black, 1 fuchsia, and 1 orange. Using leaf pattern, cut 4 medium green and 6 dark green.

Cut 2¼''-wide dark-green band long enough to fit around crown of hat plus 1'' for overlap.

Using pins to hold leaves and flowers in place until thoroughly dry, make 4 flowers, 1 each in fuchsia, beige, coral, and orange, all with black centers, as follows:

To Make Flower: Pinch and roll center petal to form middle of flower; glue to hold shape. Fold 1 outer petal in half, roll around black center, and glue at lower edge. Place this piece in center of second matching outer petal, pinch together at lower edge, and glue to hold shape. Make 3 more flowers in same manner.

To Make Bud: Pinch and roll orange or fuchsia center petal same as for the middle of large flower, and glue to hold shape. Place a dark-green leaf around bud with bud extended slightly above top of leaf; then roll leaf around lower part of bud to form stem and glue in place.

Glue band around hat. Folding each leaf in cornucopia shape, and starting at center front of hat, glue 2 dark-green leaves and 2 medium green leaves on band. Glue remaining leaves on brim as shown in photograph.

Center and glue 4 flowers between leaves. Glue 1 bud on each side of center group on brim.

MULE SLIPPERS

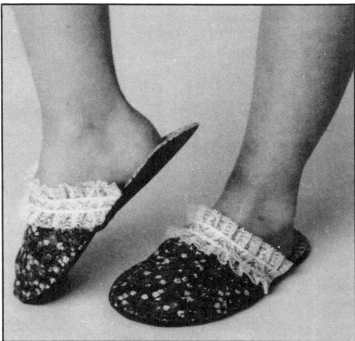

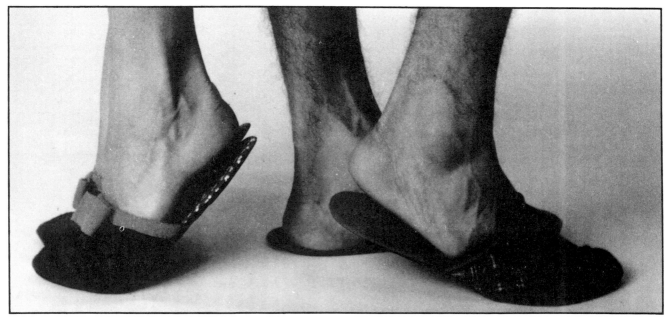

A classic cloth slipper for women, men, or children can be made from almost any fabric, according to individual taste. We chose calico, velour terry, and tartan plaid, each with appropriate trim and a sturdy base of latex insoles covered in a coordinated solid color or print.

24

GENERAL DIRECTIONS

INSOLE: 2 pairs of Dr. Scholl's Air-Pillo® Insoles (or similar quality insoles) in desired size for each pair of slippers.

For child's insole, cut adult's size to fit.

SOLE: For pattern, trace around insole on paper, adding ¼″ all around to compensate for insole thickness, then ½″ more all around for seam allowance. Mark X on each side of narrow part of insole for position of uppers. Cut 1 sole bottom and 1 lining for each foot.

With right sides together, stitch 2 matching soles around heel between X's. Clip seam and turn. For each foot, insert 2 insoles between bottom and lining; baste bottom and lining together around front part of insole with seam allowance extended outward.

UPPER: Transfer pattern to tracing paper, adding ½″ for seam allowance all around. (Patterns are for largest size in each

Full-size Patterns for Mule Uppers

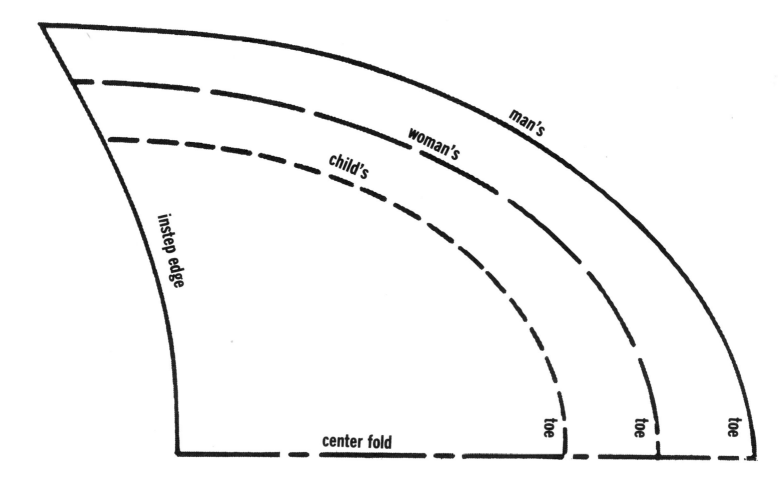

group; trim later, if necessary.) Cut one upper and one lining for each foot.

With right sides together, stitch upper to lining along instep edge. Clip seam and turn. Pin upper around front section of sole from X to X to check fit. Cut away excess if necessary, being sure to leave about ½" seam allowance.

ASSEMBLY: With right side of upper facing sole bottom, baste all 4 layers together around front section; stitch. Cut bias tape into 4 equal lengths. Fold a strip over first 3" of seam allowance on each side of foot and hand-sew to cover seam allowance. Pink or overcast remaining seam allowance around toe. Turn slipper right side out.

WOMAN'S MULE
See General Directions for Mule.

SIZES: Fits up to size 9.

MATERIALS: ¼ yard velour terry fabric for upper; ¼ yard calico for sole and upper linings; ¼ yard cotton suede for sole bottom; 1¼ yards 1⅛"-wide foldover braid; 12" bias tape to match lining; matching sewing thread.

Note: Use velour side of terry for right side of uppers. Before assembly, fold braid in half lengthwise over instep edge of upper and stitch in place. Make small braid bow and tack to front (see photograph).

MAN'S MULE
See General Directions for Mule.

SIZES: Fits up to size 11.

MATERIALS: ⅜ yard plaid woolen-type fabric for uppers; ¼ yard cotton suede in coordinating color for sole and upper linings; ¼ yard cotton suede in dark color for sole bottom; ¾ yard ½"-wide trim; 12" bias tape to match lining; matching sewing thread.

Note: Cut uppers so plaid design is centered on toe and is on the bias (see photograph). Topstitch trim along instep edge before assembly.

CHILD'S MULE
See General Directions for Mule.

SIZES: Fits up to 8½" foot.

MATERIALS: ¼ yard calico upper and upper lining; ¼ yard contrasting print calico for sole lining; ¼ yard cotton suede for sole bottom; ¾ yard lace-trimmed decorative ribbon; 12" bias tape to match lining; matching sewing thread.

Topstitch trim along instep edge before assembly.

Tool-pocket Apron

Eight storage compartments of varying sizes and shapes hold tools and utensils for a cook, carpenter, or handyperson. We made it in businesslike tan twill, but we can easily imagine a lighthearted version with every pocket a different color or print.

Instructions on following pages >

TOOL-POCKET APRON

SIZE: One size fits all adults.

MATERIALS: 1 yard 45"-wide tan brushed-twill fabric; dark-brown sewing thread.

Enlarge pattern (see How to Enlarge Patterns, page 6). Using pattern, cut apron from fabric, adding 1" all around for hems. Fold over double hem at side edges; topstitch twice, using dark-brown thread. Repeat to topstitch top and bottom.

From fabric, cut 1 each 5" x 7" three-part top pocket, 10" x 12" pleated bottom left pocket, 6" x 10" three-part lower right pocket, and 4" x 10" shallow bottom right pocket. Fold over double hem at top edge of each pocket; topstitch twice.

Position three-part top pocket centered and 6½" down from top edge of apron. Fold under raw edges and topstitch to apron along sides and bottom edges with double row of topstitching. Divide pocket into 3 parts and stitch divisions with 2 rows of stitching. Position pleated pocket next, forming ½" inverted pleats at side edges. Stitch pocket in place with double topstitching. Align three-part lower right pocket with top edges of left pocket. Stitch. Divide pocket into 3 parts and stitch divisions as for top pocket. Add shallow pocket, aligning it on bottom right corner. Stitch.

Cut three 3" x 25" strips from remaining fabric for neck piece and ties. Fold each strip in half lengthwise, right side out and raw edges tucked in; topstitch all around outside edges. Pin neck ends to each end to top edge of apron; stitch in place. Stitch a tie at each side of apron.

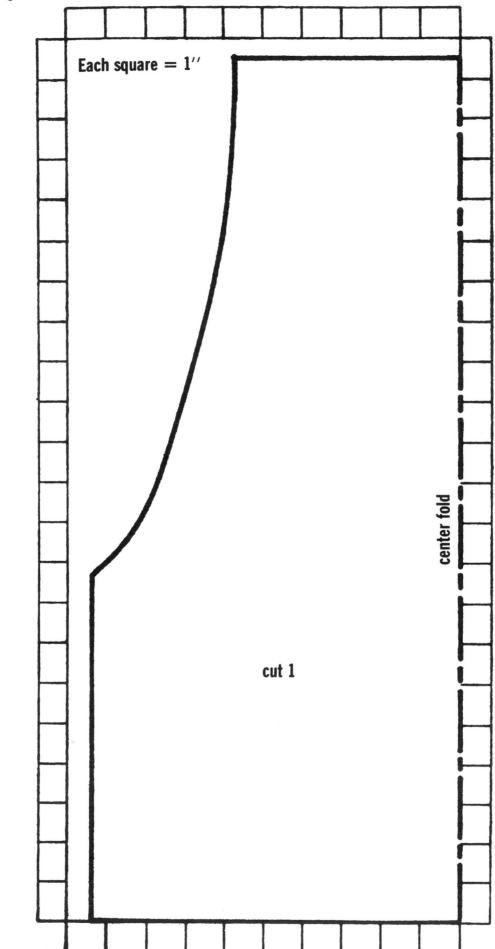

Each square = 1″

center fold

cut 1

Soft-sculpture Truck

What fun for a toddler! The removable dumper is attached with snag-loop fasteners, and since the truck has no sharp edges, it can even be parked under the covers at bedtime. Make it using any sturdy, closely woven cotton or cotton-blend scraps.

SIZE: About 12″ high x 25″ long.

MATERIALS: (**Note:** All fabrics, except metallic, should be sturdy, closely woven cotton or cotton/polyester blend, 45″ wide.) 1 yard red fabric, ½ yard blue, ⅝ yard each yellow and yellow print, ¼ yard black-and-white striped, ⅝ yard red-and-white checked gingham, 10″ square of red print; ¼ yard gold metallic fabric; matching sewing threads; three 1″ x 4″ strips Velcro fasteners; polyester-fiberfill stuffing.

TRUCK BODY: Enlarge pattern (see How to Enlarge Patterns, page 6). Cut 2 sides of truck from red fabric, reversing pattern for 1 side, and adding ½″ to all edges for seam allowance. Cut one 9½″ x 25″ red piece for top of truck, one 9″ x 9½″ red print piece for front, one 4″ x 9½″ piece each black-and-white striped and blue for radiator, one 9½″ x 28½″ gingham piece for bottom and back end. Stitch all these pieces into long strip.

Stitch around sides of truck, as follows: Making ½″ seams throughout, stitch red print to red (seam A), black-and-white striped to red print (B), blue to striped (C), and gingham to blue (D). With right sides facing, pin strip around 1 side piece, starting with end of red piece at E. Pin seam A at dot A, seam B at dot B and so on. Stitch seam. Pin and stitch other edge of strip to other side piece. Turn right side out at E. **For windows (make 3):** From yellow cut one 3½″ x 9½″ piece and two 3½″ x 5½″. Fold in raw edges (shape 1 corner on side windows as in photograph) and blindstitch to truck. With red thread, machine-zigzag-stitch through windows for divider lines.

For Wheels (make 4): From blue cut eight 7″-diameter circles. From gold cut four 3″-diameter circles. Zigzag-stitch gold circles to centers of 4 blue circles. Cut 2½″-wide striped strip to fit around a plain blue circle; stitch. Stitch other edge of strip to blue circle with gold center, leaving 4″ opening. Turn right side out and stuff. Close opening. Sew wheels securely to sides of truck.

For Lights: From gold and red fabrics cut two 4″-diameter circles each. Stitch a red to a gold for 2 lights, leaving 2″ opening. Turn and close opening. Sew to striped front of truck.

Stuff truck firmly and close back opening at E.

DUMPER: For outside of dumper, cut two 10½″ x 11½″ yellow pieces and two 11½″ x 13″ yellow print pieces for sides, and one 10½″ x 13″ yellow print bottom piece. Stitch the 11½″ edges of 4 side pieces together, alternating solids and prints, to form strip of 4 panels. For inside of dumper, from gingham cut 1 piece same size as strip and one 10½″ x 13″ bottom piece.

With right sides facing, stitch gingham and panel strips together across long edges to form tube. Turn right side out and pin 1 end of tube. Stuff to top of 1st section and pin along seam; repeat for 2nd and 3rd; stuff 4th section. Turn in and press raw ends of tube; remove pins from other end and insert into pressed end. Topstitch to form square. Topstitch along pinned sections. Stitch the 2 bottom pieces together, leaving opening. Turn and stuff lightly. Close opening. With gingham side out, making ⅛" seam, stitch bottom to square; turn.

Sew 3 Velcro strips to dumper and to back of truck.

Each square = 1″

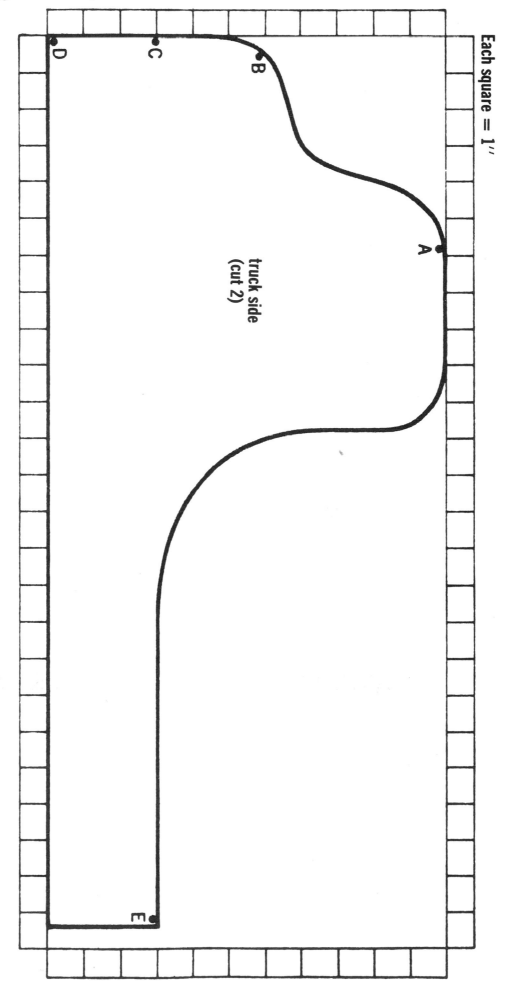

truck side
(cut 2)

HENNY-PENNY BUN WARMER

Both wings lift up for access to the warm buns she's nesting on. Her body of quilted gingham has an elasticized bottom to fit snugly over an oval store-bought basket.

Patterns to Enlarge for Henny-Penny Bun Warmer

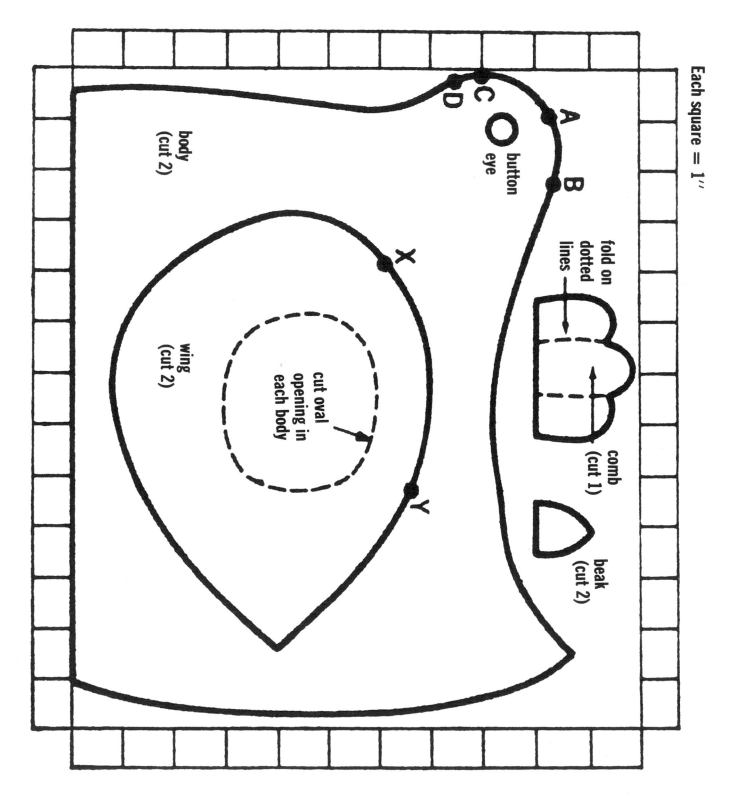

Each square = 1"

HENNY-PENNY BUN WARMER

SIZE: 8″ high.

MATERIALS: ½ yard 36″-wide quilted light-blue-and-white gingham fabric; 3 yards 1″-wide red cotton bias tape; scraps of red and yellow felt; two ½″-diameter bright-blue buttons; matching sewing thread; ½ yard ¼″-wide elastic; 3″ x 9″ oval purchased basket.

Enlarge patterns for body and wing (see How to Enlarge Patterns, page 6). Using patterns, cut 2 each body and wings, adding ½″ seam allowance to body pieces only. Cut out oval opening in each body piece as indicated by dotted lines on pattern. Finish raw edges of oval openings and both wings with red bias tape; topstitch. Pin a wing to each body piece, wrong side of wing facing right side of body; stitch between dots X and Y.

Enlarge patterns for comb and beak; cut out comb from red felt and beak from yellow. Pleat red comb as indicated by dotted lines; stitch to hold. With right sides facing, pin body together, inserting comb between dots A and B and beak pieces pinched in half lengthwise between dots C and D. Stitch around sides and top edges, leaving bottom open. Clip curves and turn.

Fold up ½″ bottom hem; stitch, leaving opening for elastic. Insert and work 1 end of elastic through hem; join ends and stitch securely. Close opening. Add eyes to each side of head as indicated. Arrange hen over basket as in photograph.

Flat-footed Pillow Creatures

With foolish faces sewn to floppy feet, they're good for a laugh and a cuddle and also for using up an assortment of solids, prints, and what-have-you. The free-form features are machine-appliquéd.

Instructions on following pages ❯

FLAT-FOOTED PILLOW CREATURES

SIZE: About 9½'' tall.

MATERIALS: Printed and plain cotton fabrics: ⅜ yard 36''-wide fabric for body, ¼ yard for feet, scraps for features; ¼ yard interfacing for feet; assorted colors sewing threads to appliqué features; polyester-fiberfill stuffing. Transfer patterns to tracing paper and cut out. Cut body from fabric and feet from fabric and interfacing, adding ½'' seam allowance to all edges.

Place tracing paper over 1 body piece and, following photograph, draw free-form features (don't try to make perfect circles and ovals; the features are funnier if they're a little crooked). Note that eyes are layered—1 circle over another. Also, nose on 1 creature is composed of 2 diamonds, 1 overlapping the other slightly. Using tracing-paper drawings as patterns, cut features from fabric scraps but do not add seam allowances. Pin features in place. Using matching or contrasting-color threads, machine zigzag-stitch closely around edges of each piece. Or appliqué by hand in ⅛''-wide satin stitch (see diagram, page 8).

Full-size Patterns for Flat-footed Pillow Creatures

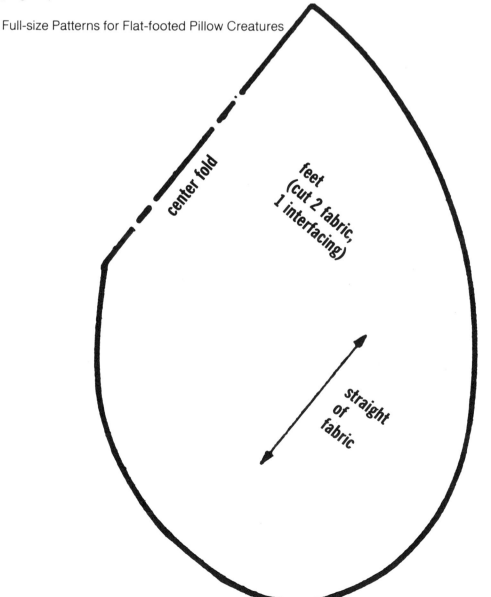

With right sides facing, stitch body front and back together around curved edges (leave bottom open). Clip seam allowance and turn. Stuff firmly. Seat creature on tracing paper and draw an oval around open end. Using drawing as pattern, cut fabric oval, adding ½″ seam allowance. Turning edges under, blindstitch oval to bottom of body.

Baste interfacing to wrong side of 1 foot piece. With right sides facing, sew foot pieces together, leaving opening for turning. Clip all seam allowances; trim seam allowance on interfacing. Turn; close opening. Topstitch ⅛″ from edge around feet.
Sew feet to base.

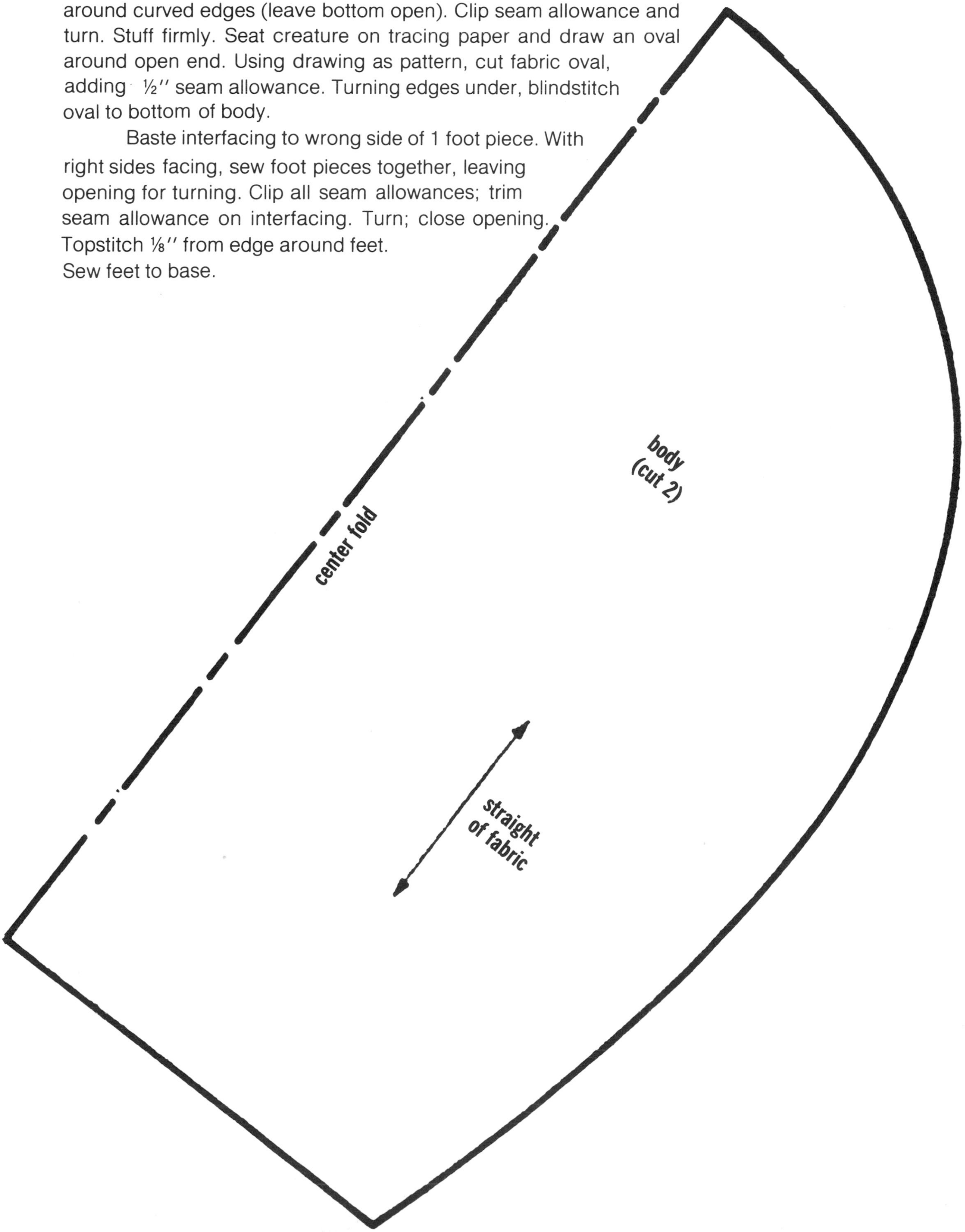

center fold

body
(cut 2)

straight
of fabric

Heart Mini Bag

Slightly padded and stitched for a quilted effect, the bag's all done by machine. In red satin, with a thick soutache cord to hang around neck and shoulder, it makes an eye-catching accessory.

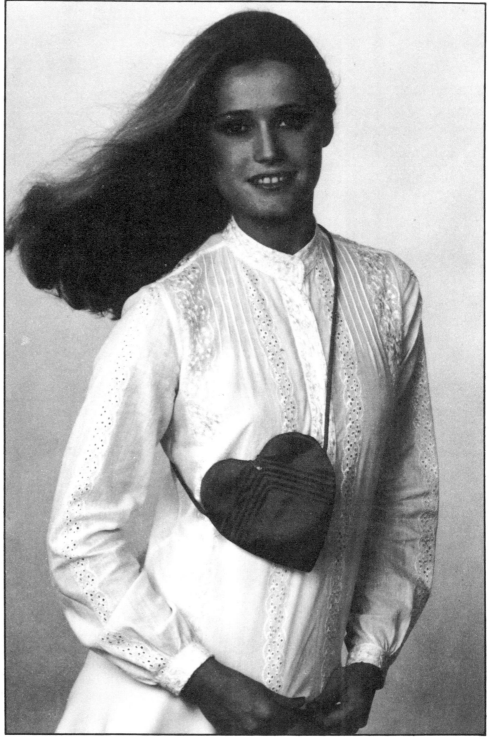

40

SIZE: 6″ x 6″.

MATERIALS: ¼ yard 36″-wide red satin; 14″ square piece of flannel or felt for soft interlining; red sewing thread; 1¼ yards thick red soutache braid; 2½″ narrow red cord; red heart button.

Transfer pattern to tracing paper and cut out. Cut out 4 full hearts from satin and 2 from interlining, adding ¼″ to all edges for seam allowance. Baste interlining hearts to wrong sides of 2 of the satin hearts.

Topstitch along broken lines on both assembled hearts for quilting detail. With right sides facing, stitch assembled hearts together around lower point from dot to other dot. Clip interlining seam allowance to ⅛″. Turn.

For bag lining, with right sides facing, stitch other 2 single hearts together around lower point from dot to dot. Insert lining in purse. Clip seam allowance on curved lobes, turn in edges and baste. Insert and pin ends of thick soutache braid in bag seams at dots. For button loop, insert and pin ends of narrow cord into seam on 1 side (back) of bag at circles. Blindstitch basted seam around lobes. Sew button to front of bag.

Full-size Patterns for Heart Mini Bag

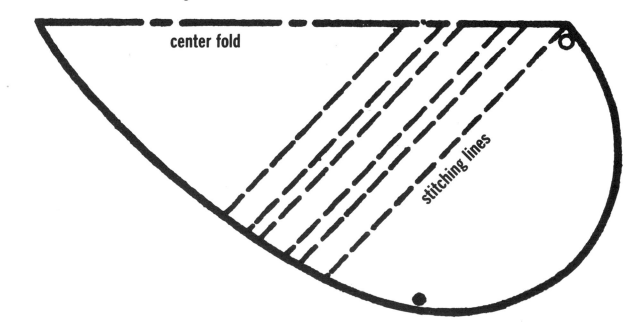

center fold

stitching lines

PUP, BUNNY, AND BEAR CUDDLERS

A trio of friendly animals offer tummies to tickle and bells to jingle (not for children under three years old, though). We used knit velour fabrics to make the "pelts" especially strokable.

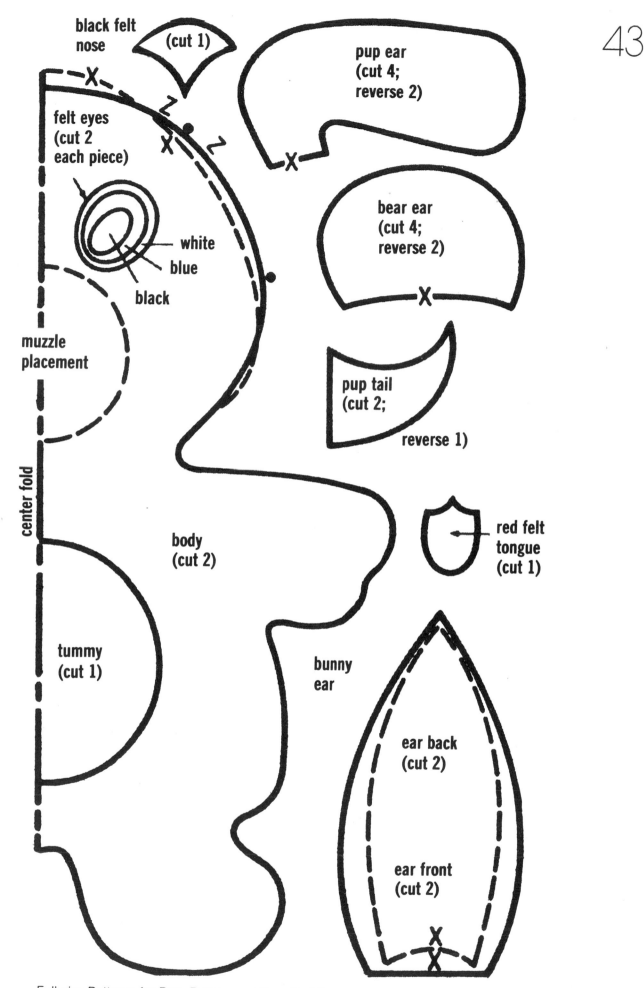

43

black felt nose (cut 1)

pup ear (cut 4; reverse 2)

felt eyes (cut 2 each piece)

white
blue
black

bear ear (cut 4; reverse 2)

muzzle placement

pup tail (cut 2; reverse 1)

center fold

red felt tongue (cut 1)

body (cut 2)

tummy (cut 1)

bunny ear

ear back (cut 2)

ear front (cut 2)

Full-size Patterns for Pup, Bunny, and Bear Cuddlers

PUP, BUNNY, AND BEAR CUDDLERS

SIZE: About 10″ from head to toe.

MATERIALS: For each toy: ⅜ yard 45″-wide knit velour fabric; scraps of pink velour for bunny's tummy and ear fronts; scraps of white fur fabric for pup's and bear's tummy; scraps of felt for eyes, nose, teeth (bunny), and tongue; matching sewing thread; 6-strand black embroidery floss for mouth; ½ yard satin ribbon; polyester-fiberfill stuffing; optional small bell (not advisable if toy is for a small child); fabric glue.

PATTERNS: Transfer patterns to tracing paper and cut out, adding ½″ to all edges for seam allowance. (Do not add to felt pieces.) For head, follow solid line for pup and bear and broken line for bunny. Cut out fabric pieces. Also cut 3″-diameter velour circle for muzzle and for bear's and bunny's tail.

STITCHING: Turn under seam allowance and appliqué tummy to front. Sew running stitches around bunny's and bear's tail piece ¼″ from edge, draw up to form pouch, stuff, and sew to body back. For pup's tail, stitch pieces together, right sides facing, leaving straight end to body back.

Turn under ¼″ around muzzle and appliqué to face, stuffing as you go. Stack and glue eye pieces together. Embroider white French knot (see diagram, page 7) to center. Glue eyes to face. Following photograph for placement, appliqué nose to muzzle and embroider mouth in outline stitch. Glue tongue to bear and pup; cut two ½″-square white felt teeth and glue to bunny.

For bear's and pup's ears, stitch matching ear pieces together, leaving edge X open. For bunny's ears stitch fronts to backs, leaving edge X open, then pleat edge X slightly on ear front. Turn all ears and pad lightly. Place ears on body front, matching raw edges to raw edges of head between dots for bear, X's for bunny, and Z's for pup; pin. Stitch body pieces together, ears sandwiched between, leaving opening on one side. Turn and stuff. Close opening. Tie bow around neck and sew on bell if desired.

POPPY PILLOW

This cheerful accessory could brighten almost any room. The flowering plant is machine-appliquéd to hopsacking for a homespun look. Solid-color heavy cotton is used for the pillow back.

Instructions on following pages ❯

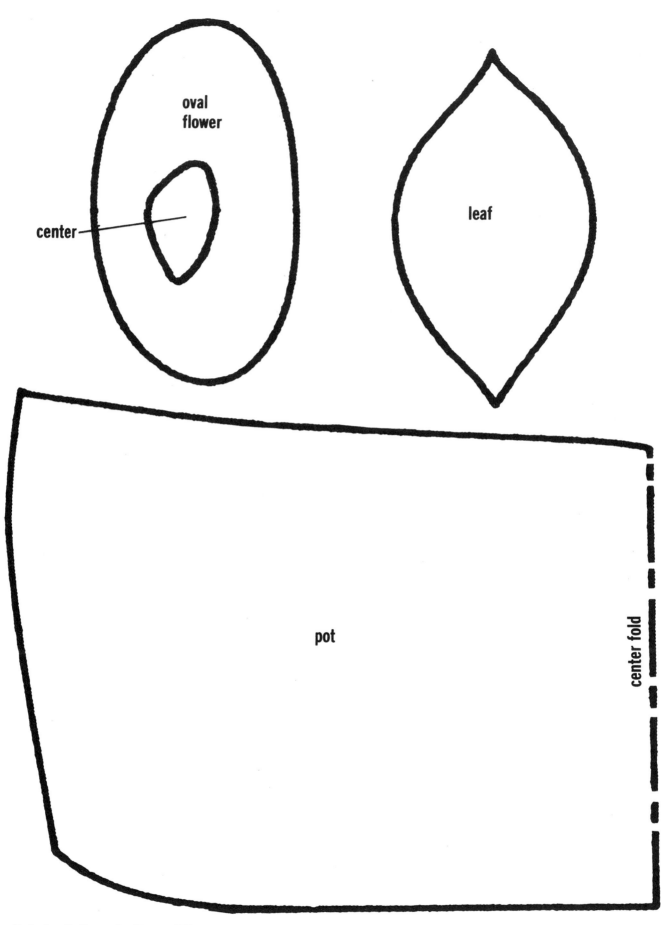

oval
flower

center

leaf

pot

center fold

Full-size Patterns for Poppy Pillow

46

POPPY PILLOW

SIZE: 16" square.

MATERIALS: 45"-wide heavy cotton fabric, ½ yard red, 6" square black, 6" x 14" piece light green, 12" square medium green; 17" square light brown hopsacking; sewing threads a shade darker than fabrics; 16" pillow form.

Transfer patterns to tracing paper and cut out. From red fabric cut 17" square (back piece), 5 oval flowers from pattern, and 4 irregular circular flowers about 4" in diameter. From black cut centers for 5 oval flowers from pattern and 4 irregular centers about 1½" in diameter for circular flowers. From medium green cut 7 leaves from pattern and rectangles measuring ⅝"x 2½", ⅝" x 3", and ⅝" x 4" for stems. From light green cut pot using pattern.

Following photograph, pin appliqué pieces to hopsacking. Sew to hopsacking, using wide zigzag machine stitching. Or sew by hand, using satin or button stitch (see diagrams, page 7) around edges of pieces. Work detail lines on leaves, flowers, and pot (see photograph) in same manner.

With right sides facing, using ½" seams, sew top and back pieces together along 3 sides. Turn, insert pillow form, and blindstitch opening.

Doll-face Bookends

A redhead and a blonde with beautiful big eyes and pouty mouths lend their charms to fancy slipcovers that fit the plain metal bookends you can buy in stationery and variety stores. The stuffed cotton heads have felt hair and features and are tacked to felt sleeves.

MATERIALS: 4¾"-square purchased metal bookends; 17" square white cotton fabric; felt, one 12" square each red-orange, yellow-orange, yellow, and turquoise; small amounts felt in white, brown, rose, and royal blue; 12" piece of 1"-wide pregathered white cotton eyelet lace; small amount polyester-fiberfill stuffing; matching sewing thread.

Note: To sew felt pieces, use doubled matching sewing threads.

Transfer patterns to tracing paper and cut out.

BLONDE: From white cotton fabric cut two 7½"-diameter circles for head (½" seam allowance included). Using patterns, cut 4 yellow-orange felt hair pieces, 2 royal-blue eyelids, 2 white eye pieces, and 1 red-orange mouth. For eyeball circles cut 2 each ½" royal-blue and ¾" turquoise. For bookend cover cut from turquoise one 5" square and one 5" x 7" piece, curving corners to match bookends.

With right sides facing, sew white head circles together, leaving

Full-size Patterns for Doll-face Bookends

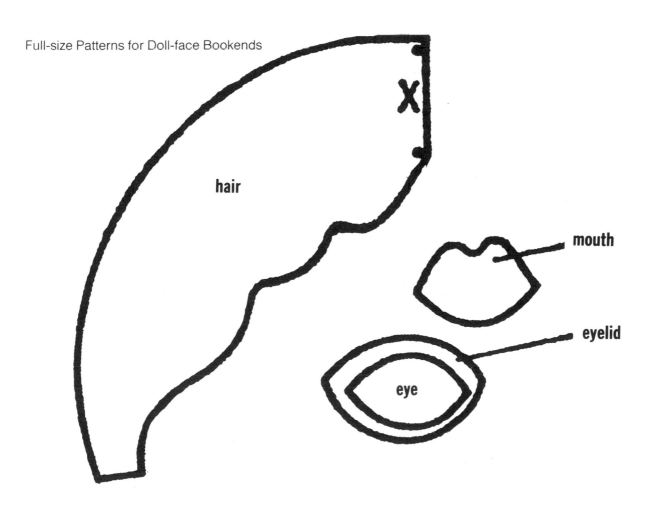

hair

X

mouth

eyelid

eye

4″ opening (chin edge); clip seam, turn. Sew 2 hair pieces together by overcasting edge X between dots to form front hair section. Sew other 2 pieces together to form back hair section. Pin hair sections to head and sew all layers together using blanket stitch, (see diagram, page 7), along outside edge.

For each eye, overcast eye white to eyelid. Center royal-blue circle on turquoise circle and sew to eye with a royal-blue French knot (see diagram, page 7) at center. Following photograph, overcast eyes to head. Work long stitches along top for lashes.

Following photograph, sew on mouth and work 2 royal-blue French knots for nostrils.

Stuff head and stitch closed, gathering in to shape chin if desired. Sew 6″ length of lace at chin.

Tack head at one end of 5″ x 7″ shaped felt piece. Line up 5″ square at wrong side of same end and blanket-stitch pieces together around 3 sides so that completed piece forms a sleeve to fit over bookend.

REDHEAD: Work same as for blonde, making red-orange hair, brown eyelids, rose mouth, and yellow bookend cover.

Boat Slippers

There's a fit for everyone in the family: from little toddler to adult women and men, and you can use almost any fabric that comes to hand (calico, gingham, and pseudo-suede are shown here). All slippers except the infant's have a covered latex innersole.

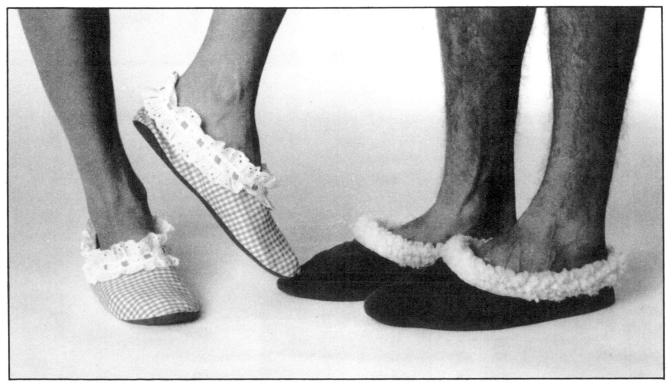

Instructions on following pages >

BOAT SLIPPERS

GENERAL DIRECTIONS

INSOLE: 2 pairs Dr. Scholl's Air-Pillo® Insoles (or similar quality insole) in desired size for each pair of slippers (except for infant's). For child's insole, cut down an adult size to fit.

SOLE: For pattern, trace around insole on paper, adding ¼" all around to compensate for sole thickness, and add ½" more all around for seam allowance when cutting. Use pattern for infant's sole. Cut 1 sole bottom and 1 lining for each foot.

For each foot, place 2 insoles between bottom and lining, wrong sides of fabric facing. Pin and baste all around insoles, with seam allowance extended outward.

UPPER: Transfer pattern to tracing paper, extending sides of uppers to center back of heel, and adding ½" all around for seam allowance. (Patterns for uppers are for largest size in each group; trim later, if necessary). Cut 1 upper and 1 upper lining for each foot.

With right sides together, stitch upper to lining around top edge; seam back edges of upper (not lining). Clip seams and turn, then turn in seam allowance on back edge of lining and blindstitch.

ASSEMBLY: With right side of upper facing sole bottom, baste all 4 layers together; stitch. Pink or overcast seam allowance. Turn slipper right side out. Sew trim around top edge.

Note: If tighter fit around top edge of slipper is desired, add a strip of ¼"-wide elastic around inner top edge.

WOMAN'S BOAT

See General Directions for Boat.

SIZES: Fits up to size 9.

MATERIALS: ¼ yard checkered cotton for uppers; ½ yard striped cotton for sole linings and upper linings; ¼ yard cotton-suede fabric for sole bottoms; 1 yard 2"-wide eyelet trim with beading; 1 yard double-fold bias tape to weave through beading slots; matching sewing thread.

Note: Lace tape through eyelet trim; sew trim around top edge of each slipper, overlapping ends at center back.

MAN'S BOAT

See General Directions for Boat.

SIZES: Fits up to size 11.

MATERIALS: ½ yard cotton-suede fabric for uppers and sole

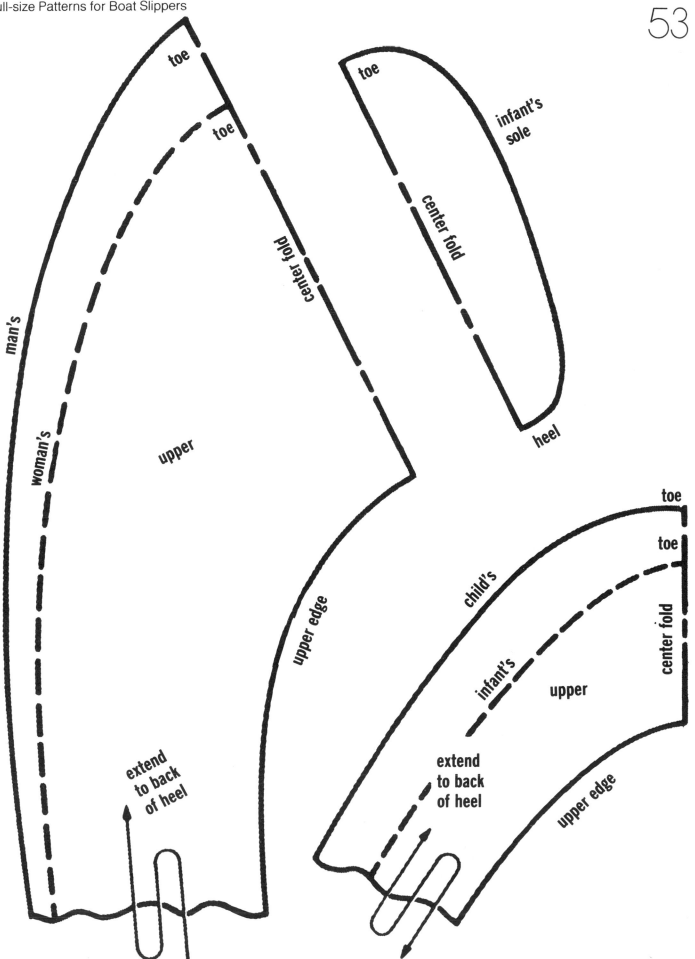

bottoms; ½ yard calico for sole linings and upper linings; ¼ yard 2''-wide fake fur fabric for trim; matching sewing thread.

Note: Cut fake fur to fit around top edge of each slipper. Fold strip in half lengthwise over edge and sew, overlapping ends at center back.

CHILD'S BOAT

See General Directions for Boat.

SIZES: Fits up to 8½'' foot.

MATERIALS: ⅜ yard cotton-suede fabric for uppers and sole bottoms; ½ yard calico for sole linings and upper linings and trim; matching sewing thread.

Note: Cut 1½''-wide bias strips of calico for trim. Fold in half lengthwise over top edge of slipper. Pin in place. Turn under ¼'' along each raw edge and stitch in place, overlapping ends at center back.

INFANT'S BOAT

See General Directions for Boat.

SIZES: Fits foot about 4'' long.

MATERIALS: ¼ yard calico for uppers and sole bottoms; ¼ yard calico in coordinating print for sole linings and upper linings; ½ yard ¾''-wide lace trim; ½ yard double-fold bias tape for trim; matching sewing thread.

Note: Insoles are not used for this slipper. Enlarge pattern for sole and cut from double fabric, adding ½'' seam allowance.

Pin bias tape to center of lace; working through both layers, stitch tape and lace trim around top edge of slipper, overlapping ends at center back.

VALENTINE PINCUSHION

With a piece of chintz, a swatch of linen, and a bit of lace you can make this pretty sewing aid. The pillow is firmly stuffed and has a pocket for small tools. Sewing scissors can be slipped under the band across the heart.

Instructions on following pages >

VALENTINE PINCUSHION

SIZE: 7" x 8½".

MATERIALS: 18" x 24" piece chintz; scrap of solid pink linen; scrap of ½"-wide lace; 5' of ½"-wide bias tape; small amount of stuffing; matching sewing thread.

Transfer heart pattern to tracing paper and cut out. Cut two 7" x 8½" and one 3" x 7" chintz pieces. Cut heart from linen, adding ½" for hem. Cut 2" x 4½" linen strip.

Bind 1 long edge of 3" x 7" chintz with bias tape; stitch; put aside. Turn under and press raw edges around heart shape. Fold linen strip to 1" width with raw edges pressed to center of wrong side. Center strip across heart, turning under raw edges at ends. Stitch strip to heart edges. Then divide strip in thirds and stitch across strip at these divisions.

Pin bias tape around heart edge; stitch in place. Make long basting stitches along raw edge of lace trim; pin lace around heart, gathering lace in slight ruffle; stitch. Position heart on one 7" x 8½" chintz piece as in photograph. Pad heart shape; stitch heart in place.

Position chintz pocket strip at bottom of front piece with bias-tape edge at top. With wrong sides facing, baste pillow together, leaving opening on one side above pocket. Lightly stuff. Bind edges with tape; stitch.

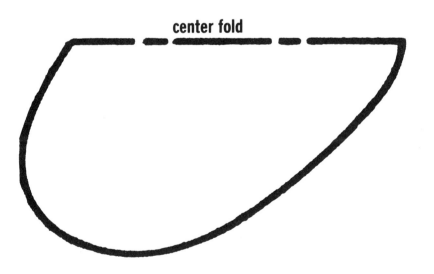

center fold

Full-size Pattern for Valentine Pincushion

Patchwork Dog Coat

Fido will look snazzy and feel cozy in a quilted coat of many colors (use patchwork fabric or piece your own from scraps). Batting is sandwiched between the surface fabric and gingham lining; neck straps and belt have convenient snag-loop fastenings.

Instructions on following pages >

PATCHWORK DOG COAT

MATERIALS: Equal amounts (see note below) of patchwork fabric, gingham fabric for lining, and quilt batting or acrylic blanketing (if desired, make patchwork fabric from assorted scraps of cotton fabric); Velcro tape fasteners for belt and neck closing; matching sewing thread; brown wrapping paper; ruler; tape measure.

Note: Take measurements of dog to make pattern. Then measure pattern to determine amount of fabric required.

TO MAKE PATTERN: Measure dog from neck to base of tail and around widest girth of body, as shown in drawing of dog. To make pattern, draw a dotted horizontal line equal to length of dog (neck-to-tail measurement) on brown paper. By folding and marking, divide this line into 16 equal parts; continue line the equivalent of 5 more parts, as indicated on our sample grid. Draw vertical line at right angle to first line. Measure down this line a distance of ¼ girth; divide into 4 equal parts. Add 1 more part below line, as on sample grid. Draw in grid from marked points. (**Note:** For a short, fat dog, you will get short, fat rectangles; for a dachshund you will get longer, narrower ones.) Following coat pattern on sample grid, transfer outline for coat rectangle by rectangle. Cut out paper pattern.

CUTTING: Cut out coat from patchwork fabric, gingham, and batting, adding ½" seam allowance to all edges. From patchwork and gingham, for belt, cut rectangle to measure 2¼" wide by dog's measurement across middle plus 4".

Baste batting to wrong side of gingham. With right sides facing, stitch patchwork and gingham-batting together, leaving 5" opening at tail end. Trim seams; clip curves; turn. Sew opening closed. Quilt in small running stitches around each patchwork shape.

With right sides facing, stitch belt pieces together, leaving opening to turn. Trim seams; turn. Blindstitch opening. Topstitch one end to lining of coat at center of one side edge.

Following manufacturer's directions, stitch Velcro tape to neck straps and end of belt and to corresponding point on opposite side of coat.

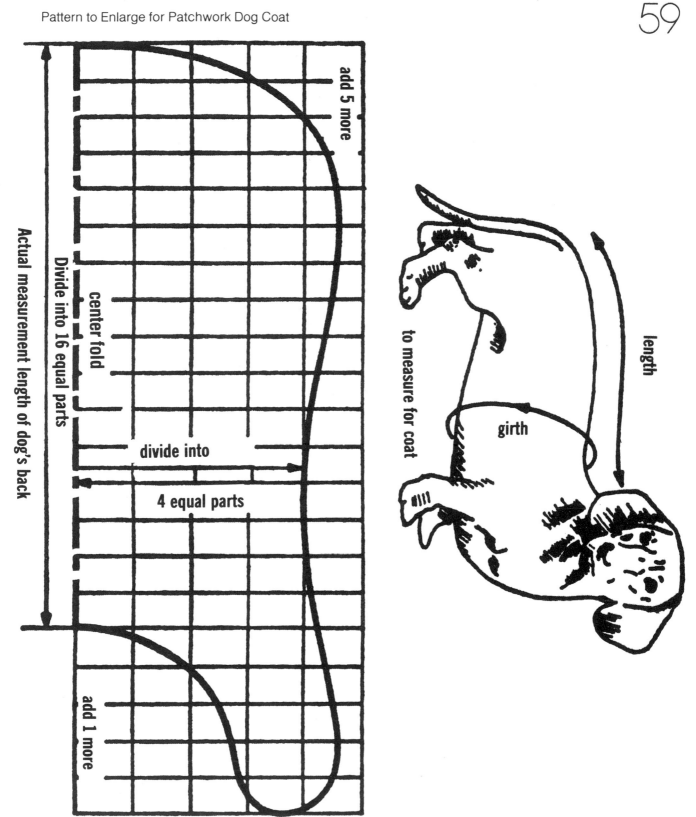

add 5 more

Actual measurement length of dog's back

Divide into 16 equal parts

center fold

divide into

4 equal parts

add 1 more

to measure for coat

length

girth

Petal Pillow

Calico scraps in eight different small floral prints form sixteen petals around a sunny yellow center. Each puffed wedge is sewn separately, so you must be a patient worker to create this unusual pillow.

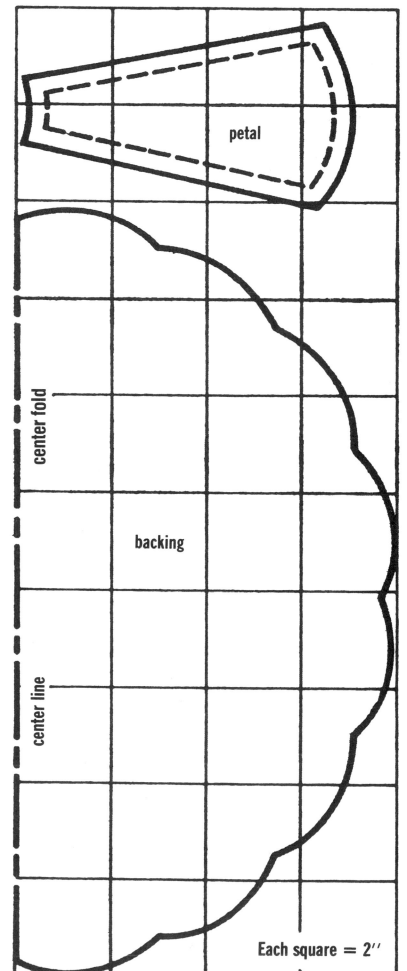

petal

center fold

center line

backing

Each square = 2″

PETAL PILLOW

SIZE: About 16″ in diameter.

MATERIALS: Scraps of printed cottons (we used 8 different small floral prints for petals and a solid color in center); 18″-square cotton print for backing; polyester-fiberfill stuffing; ½ yard 36″-wide unbleached muslin for liner; matching sewing thread.

Enlarge patterns (see How to Enlarge Patterns, page 6). Cut out, adding ½″ seam allowance all around to both pieces. Following broken lines on petal pattern, cut a pattern for petal lining, adding ½″ seam allowance. Cut two petals of each print if using 8 different prints, or cut 16 petals as desired. Cut a 5¾″-diameter solid-color-fabric circle for center. From muslin cut 16 petal linings and one 5″-diameter circle lining. From print cut backing piece.

Run a basting thread around a petal seam, drawing up thread until piece is same size as a lining piece. With wrong sides together stitch petal to lining, leaving 2″ opening for stuffing. Stuff softly so that printed side puffs up and lining is flat. Stitch opening closed on all petals. Make 15 more petals and center circle in same manner.

With right sides facing, stitch 2 petals together along adjacent long sides. Stitch 3rd petal to 2nd, then 4th to 3rd and so on until 16 petals are joined. Stitch remaining edge of 16th petal to 1st to form ring. Stitch ring to center circle. Trim seams.

With right sides facing, stitch backing to pillow front, leaving opening for turning. Turn and stuff. Blindstitch opening.

CHILD'S SHOE CADDY

Four pairs of shoes stay shipshape when they're tucked into the pockets of a heavyweight cotton caddy with a bold tugboat appliqué. Three grommets at the top allow on-the-wall hanging.

Instructions on following pages >

CHILD'S SHOE CADDY

SIZE: 16½″ x 22″.

MATERIALS: ½ yard 36″-wide natural canvas; ¼ yard 36″-wide each solid dark-green, red, and bright-blue cotton fabric, scraps solid-yellow and yellow-and-navy-blue checked cotton fabric; ½ yard 18″ iron-on bonding mesh; three ½″-diameter chrome-plated grommets; matching sewing thread.

Cut canvas to 17½″ x 26″; press ½″ hems along side edges. Enlarge patterns for ship, smoke, and portholes, (see How to Enlarge Patterns, page 6) and cut out. Using patterns, cut out a red ship, two connecting yellow-and-blue checked smoke trails, and two yellow portholes.

Following manufacturer's directions, cut bonding mesh slightly smaller than patterns. Assemble ship and bond to canvas background. (**Note:** If you do not wish to work with bonding mesh, the ship design can be machine-appliquéd to canvas. Use a close zigzag stitch to prevent raw edges from raveling.)

To make shoe pockets, enlarge pattern for waves. Cut an 8″ x 20″ piece each from blue and green cotton. Using pattern, cut one long edge for wave. Stitch ¼″ hem along edge. Press 1″ inverted pleat at center of blue and green pieces, then press ½″ pleats at sides as shown on pattern. Press ¼″ hems at side and bottom edges. Pin green pockets in place on canvas and stitch along side and bottom edges. Repeat for blue pockets, positioning so the wave slightly overlaps green and a 2½″ canvas edge is left for bottom hem.

To finish caddy cut at 2¼″ x 16½″ and a 1¼″ x 16½″ strip of bonding mesh. Fold over 1½″ hem at top of caddy, slip in 1¼″-wide bonding mesh and press. Repeat for 2½″ bottom hem. Mark placement for centered grommet and a grommet ¾″ in from each side edge along top hem of caddy. Use grommet punch to make holes; install grommets.

Patterns to Enlarge for Child's Shoe Caddy

Each square = 1"

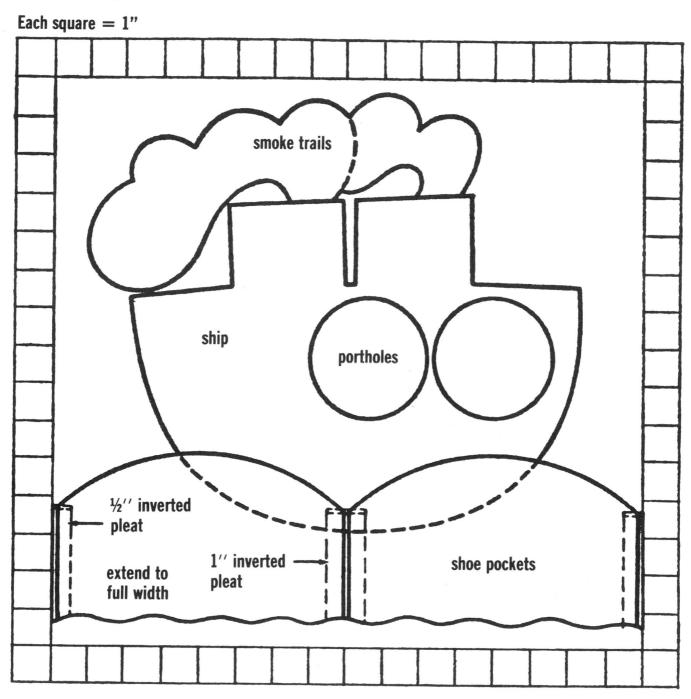

smoke trails

ship

portholes

½'' inverted pleat

extend to full width

1'' inverted pleat

shoe pockets

BUTTERFLY PLACE MAT

Coordinate the colors of the butterfly's wings with those in your kitchen or dining room. The shapes are cut from any firmly woven fabric and appliquéd by hand.

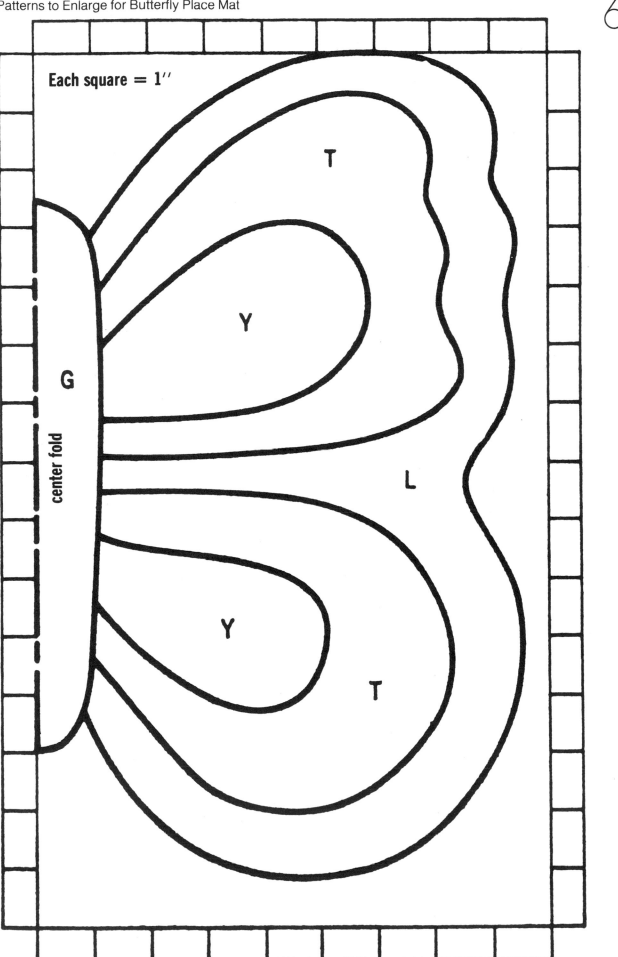

Each square = 1''

G

center fold

T

Y

L

Y

T

BUTTERFLY PLACE MAT

SIZE 14½″ x 17″.

MATERIALS: Firmly woven fabric, ¼ yard each light turquoise (color L) and turquoise (T), ½ yard each yellow (Y) and green (G); matching sewing thread.

Enlarge pattern (see How to Enlarge Patterns, page 6). Add ½″ seam allowance; cut out butterfly shape from L, 2 each of upper and lower T sections, 2 each of upper and lower Y sections, and 1 center G section.

Turn under seam allowances, clipping curves as necessary. Following photograph, appliqué pieces by hand to L butterfly shape, starting with T sections, then Y sections and G section. Hem outer edges.

Use spray starch to add body to soft fabrics. Spray Scotchgard on untreated fabrics to help retard stains.

Pigtail Pol Vanity

Sure to thrill a little girl:
her own good-grooming shelf
with a helpful "friend" to hold
her mirror, brush, and comb.
Some simple carpentry and
painting are called for before
you add the child's figure,
using fabric scraps, yarn,
and a dime-store mirror.

Instructions on following pages >

PIGTAIL POL VANITY

MATERIALS: One quarter sheet of ¾'' plywood, 12'' x 48''; 8''-diameter circular mirror; sheet of corrugated cardboard; 1 skein rust acrylic yarn; ½ yard calico; scrap fabrics, bias tape, eyelet, and ribbon; ½ yard of 1'' polyester padding; 3 buttons; matching sewing thread; semi-gloss latex paint in desired color for background; picture hanger.

Cut plywood back 10'' x 27'' and shelf 10'' x 16''. Butt shelf to back as shown on diagram; glue and screw together. Fill plywood edges with putty. Sand, prime, and paint with two coats of latex.

Enlarge pattern (see How to Enlarge Patterns, page 6) and cut out body outline from cardboard. Cut out calico body in same shape, plus 1'' allowance, and matching padding piece with allowance. Cut all remaining pattern pieces from fabrics, eyelet, and bias edging, adding ½'' allowance to all parts.

Cover cardboard with padding, wrapping around edges and gluing to back. Repeat with calico body piece. Sew edging to pockets and shoulder pieces, following diagram and photograph, and slip-stitch to body. Sew buttons in place as indicated on diagram.

Glue body to plywood back as shown, weighting down with heavy object until dry. Glue mirror at top. Unfold, flatten out skein of yarn, and cut through both ends (or cut 36'' pieces and place next to each other); wrap a couple of times with a length of yarn at center for part in hair. Glue yarn in place on mirror and make two braids; tie with ribbon. Mount picture hangers on back and hang on wall from screw set into anchor or other sturdy attachment.

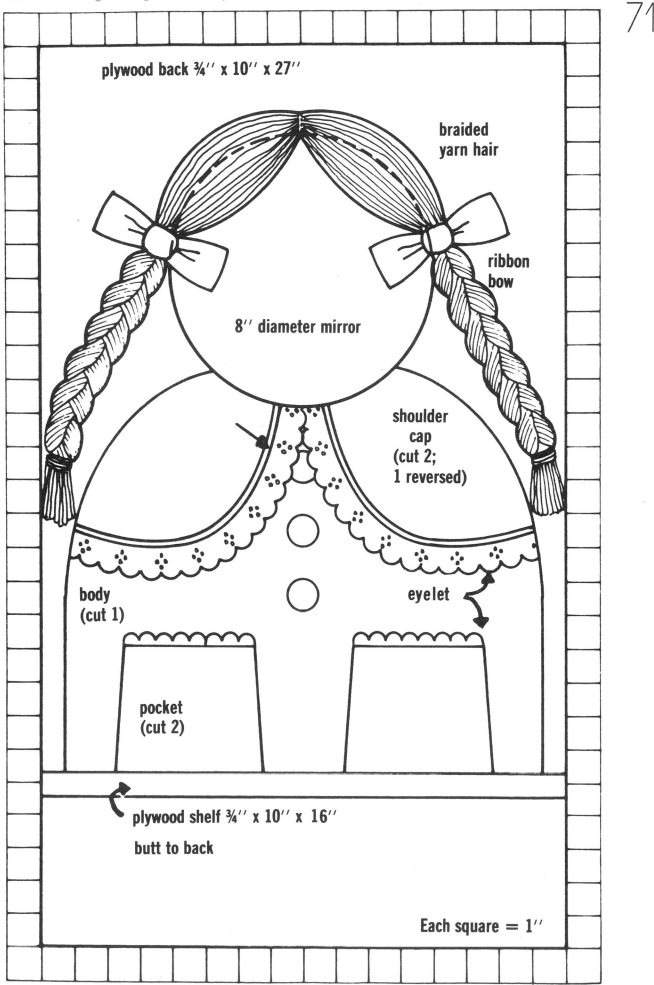

plywood back ¾'' x 10'' x 27''

braided
yarn hair

ribbon
bow

8'' diameter mirror

shoulder
cap
(cut 2;
1 reversed)

body
(cut 1)

eyelet

pocket
(cut 2)

plywood shelf ¾'' x 10'' x 16''

butt to back

Each square = 1''

Jewelry Banners

Show off your treasures and find what you want in a hurry with three fabric panels hung on a dowel that rests on two cup hooks. You attach pads for pins, vinyl pockets for earrings and rings, loops for bangles, and curtain rings for necklaces and bracelets.

SIZE: 21″ wide x 14½″ long.

MATERIALS: 18″ x 36″ piece camel felt; 18″-square piece in each pink linen-like fabric and antique gold cotton fabric; of 18″ x 18″ piece of batting; 9½ yards copper single-fold cotton bias tape; 10″ x 10″ piece clear vinyl material; six 1″-diameter brass café rings; 19″ piece ¼″-diameter dowel; two 1″-diameter wooden beads or finials; matching sewing thread; small tabs of Velcro fastener; white glue; pigmented-shellac primer; acrylic paint; two ½″-diameter screw-type cup hooks.

Extend pattern to 15″ for shorter banner pieces and 17″ for longer center piece. Using patterns, cut two each pink linen and felt pieces to 15″, then one each antiqué gold and felt piece to 17″. Cut batting pieces for two 15″ and one 17″ banner part. With right sides out, sandwich linen, batting, and felt or cotton, batting, and felt parts together.

Cut two gold and batting pieces to 4″ x 5″ for pin pads. Cut two

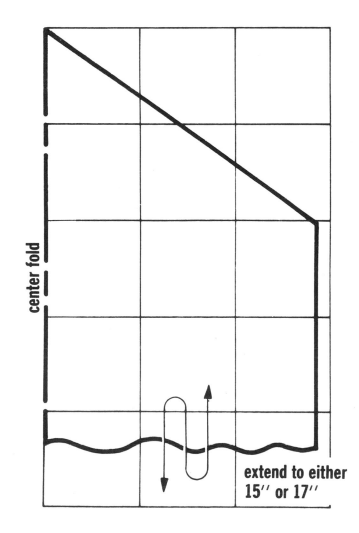

extend to either
15″ or 17″

Full-size Pattern for Jewelry Banners

2½" wide strips, one to 4½" and one to 7" lengths, from pink linen for bracelet straps.

Mark and cut clear vinyl into four 2" x 10" strips. Following photograph, fold inverted box pleats at ends and centers of strips and use masking tape to hold pleats in place. Pleat one strip for two pockets and the remaining strips for three pockets.

Center pin pads about 3" down from top edge of pink pieces. Tuck raw edges in; topstitch. Position vinyl pocket strips along bottom edge as shown on pink pieces; topstitch along sides, bottom, and between pockets.

With wrong sides together, stitch linen strips into 1"-wide strips; turn to right side. Tuck in raw edges at ends; topstitch. Following manufacturer's directions, match one end of short strip to one end of long one and position one Velcro tab on top; topstitch all three pieces centered 3" down from top edge of gold piece. Topstitch around Velcro tab, then topstitch second part of Velcro to end to short strip. Stitch remaining two Velcro tabs to long strip, one at bottom end with second tab about midway up strip.

Following photograph, hand-stitch café rings grouped in a triangular arrangement at bottom of center gold piece.

Bind all edges except tops of banner pieces with bias tape. Fold over top edges, leaving 1½"-wide casing, and topstitch.

Prime and paint dowel and finials; let dry. Slip dowel through banner casings as in photograph and glue finals in place. Use cup hooks to hang dowel.

Pelican Pajama Bag

A nonsense verse about this odd bird says, "His bill holds more than his belly can," and our pelican holds pajamas. He's especially nice to snuggle with since we chose fake-fur fabric for his body; the bill is made of felt, and the wings are lined with calico.

Instructions on following pages >

PELICAN PAJAMA BAG

SIZE: Pelican measures about 25″ high x 32″ wide.

MATERIALS: ¾ yard 60″-wide white fake-fur fabric (color W); ½ yard 36″-wide orange felt (color O); 14″ square yellow and white cotton print fabric (color P); 4″ square each yellow (color Y) and blue (color B) felt; polyester-fiberfill stuffing; fabric cement; matching sewing threads.

Enlarge patterns, (see How to Enlarge Patterns, page 6), and cut fabrics, adding ½″ to all edges for seam allowance.

Wings: With right sides facing, sew P and W together, beginning and ending ½″ below large dots and leaving straight edge open. Clip curves; turn. Sew fur side **only** to body between dots. Turn wing with print side up and, folding raw edge under, blindstitch print fabric over seam allowance.

Upper Bill: With right sides facing, stitch pieces together, leaving straight edge (between dots) open. Trim seams and turn. Firmly stuff to make rounded bill. Sew open end closed.

Lower Bill: With right sides facing, stitch pieces together, leaving top straight edge and one side between double dots open. Clip curves; turn. Turn top edge under ½″ and topstitch ¼″ from fold.
Loop: From O cut ¾″ x 5″ strip. Fold in half lengthwise and topstitch close to raw edge. Sew ends to bill at top of side seam.

Body: Sew darts. Pin body pieces together with right sides facing. Matching double dots on raw edge of lower bill to double dots on body, slide lower bill between body pieces with raw edges matching. Stitch body pieces together with lower bill sandwiched between, leaving upper-bill area (between small dots) and 6″ along bottom open. Clip curves; turn and stuff firmly. Blindstitch 6″ opening. Insert seam allowance of upper bill and, turning under raw body edges, securely blindstitch in place. Using fabric cement, glue eye pieces together, then glue eyes in place.

Patterns to Enlarge for Pelican Pajama Bag

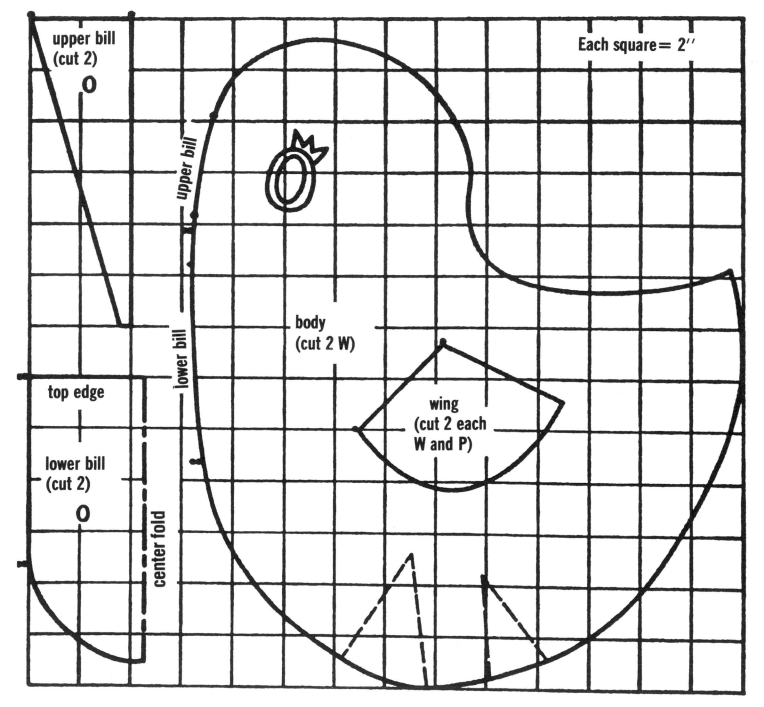

upper bill
(cut 2)

O

upper bill

Each square = 2"

lower bill

body
(cut 2 W)

top edge

wing
(cut 2 each
W and P)

lower bill
(cut 2)

O

center fold

Foxy Wall Hanging

This padded and appliquéd "family portrait" could well become the decorating focal point of a room. It's made of five panels and mixes interesting textures: velvet for the background; broadcloth with touches of satin; and fake suede for the foxes.

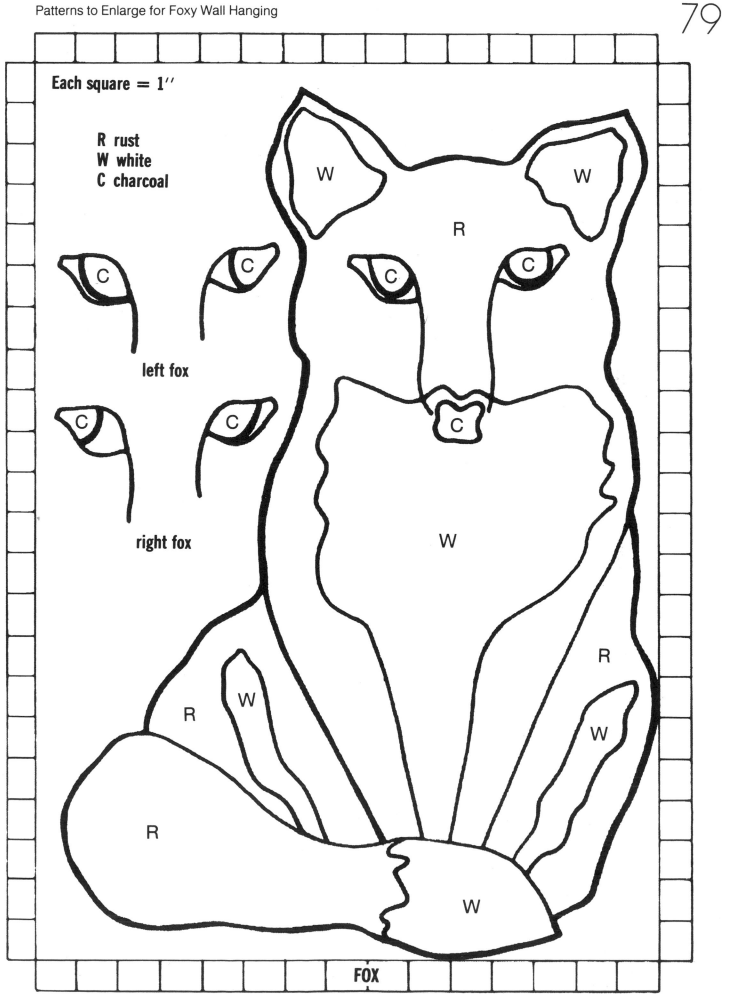

Each square = 1"

R rust
W white
C charcoal

W

W

R

C

C

C

left fox

C

C

C

right fox

W

R

W

R

W

R

W

FOX

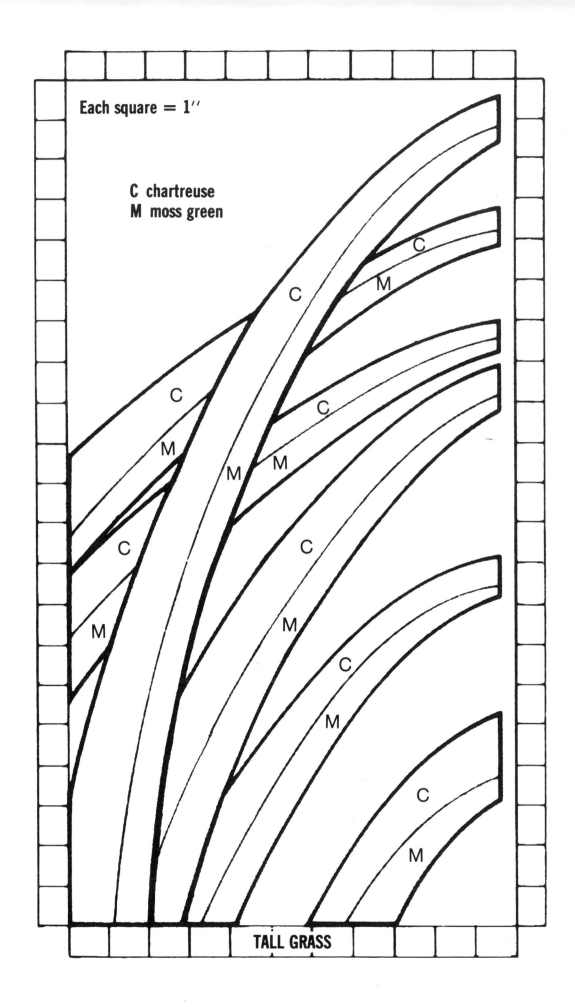

Each square = 1"

C chartreuse
M moss green

TALL GRASS

80

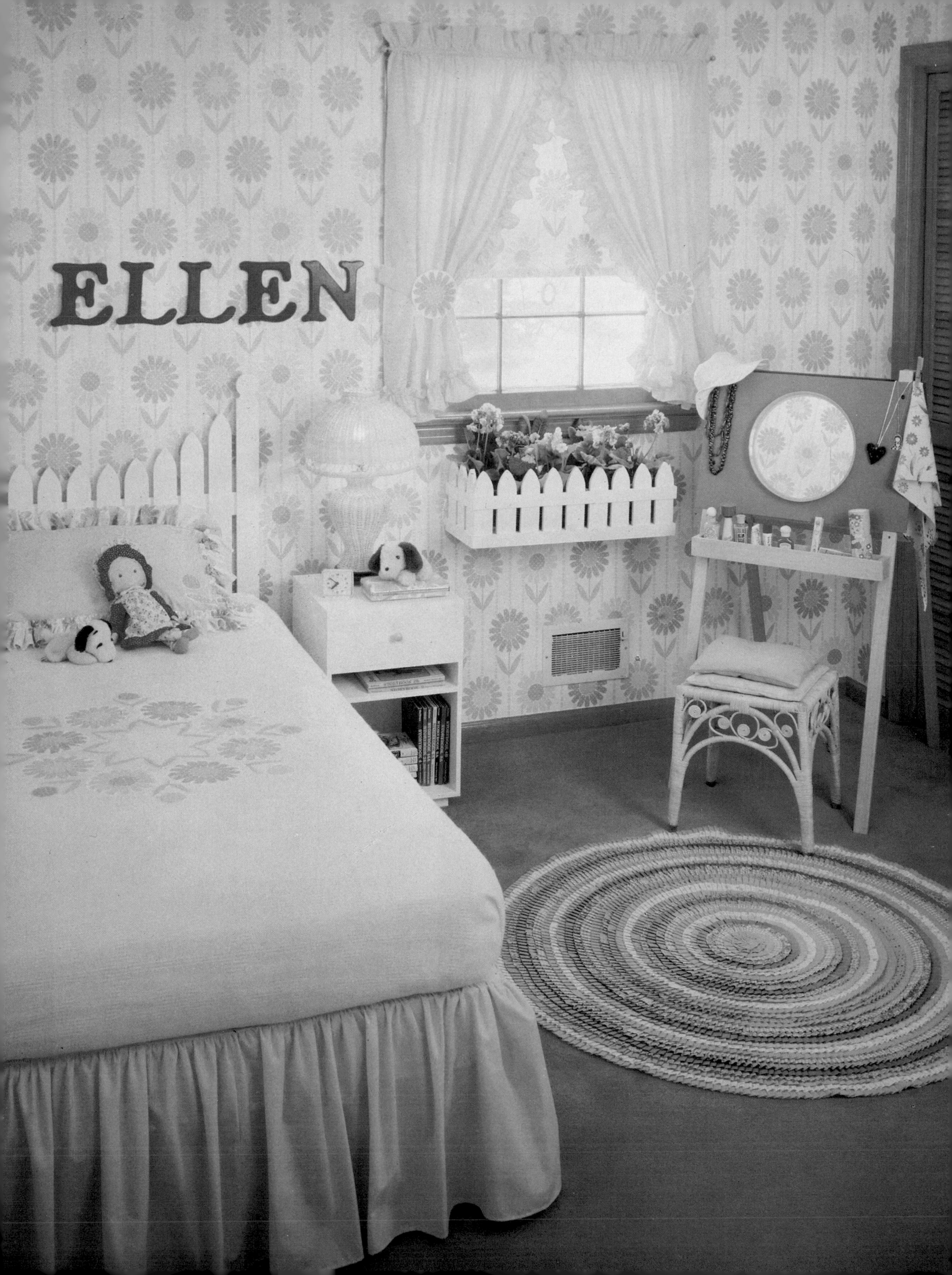
ELLEN

see page 154

see page 127

see page 45

see page 69

see page 63

see page 118

see page 11

see page 124

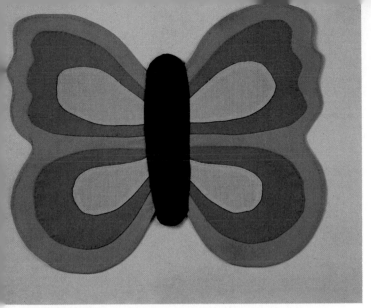

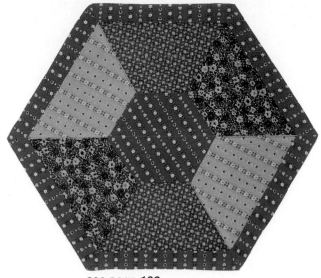

see page 66

see page 106

see page 118

see page 142

see page 148

see page 141

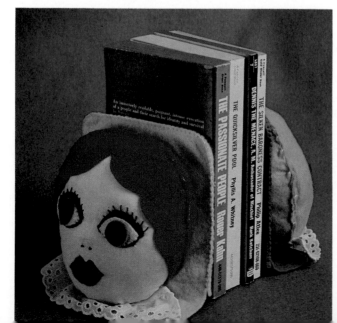

see page 48

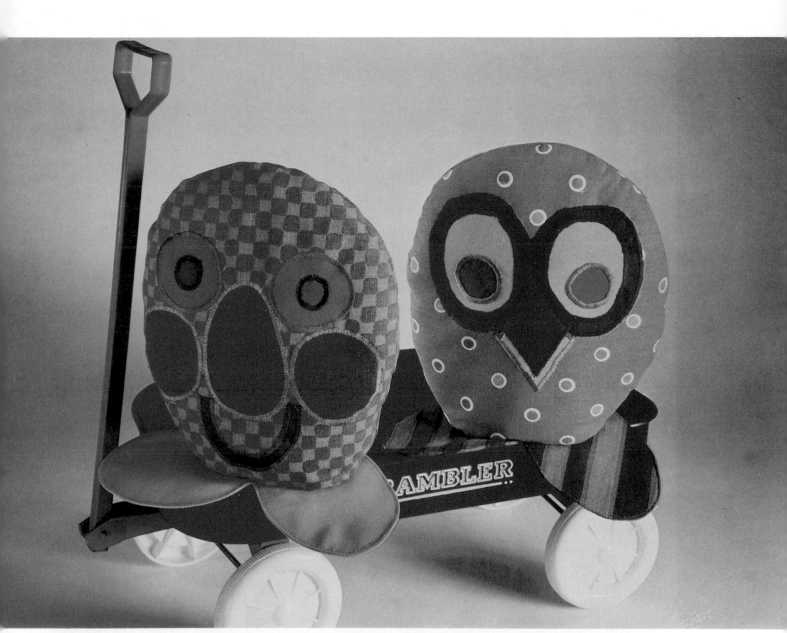

see page 37

see page 78

see page 45

see page 34

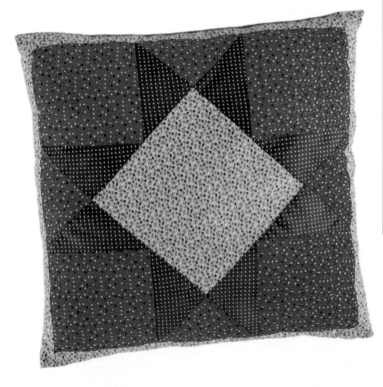

see page 133

see page 75

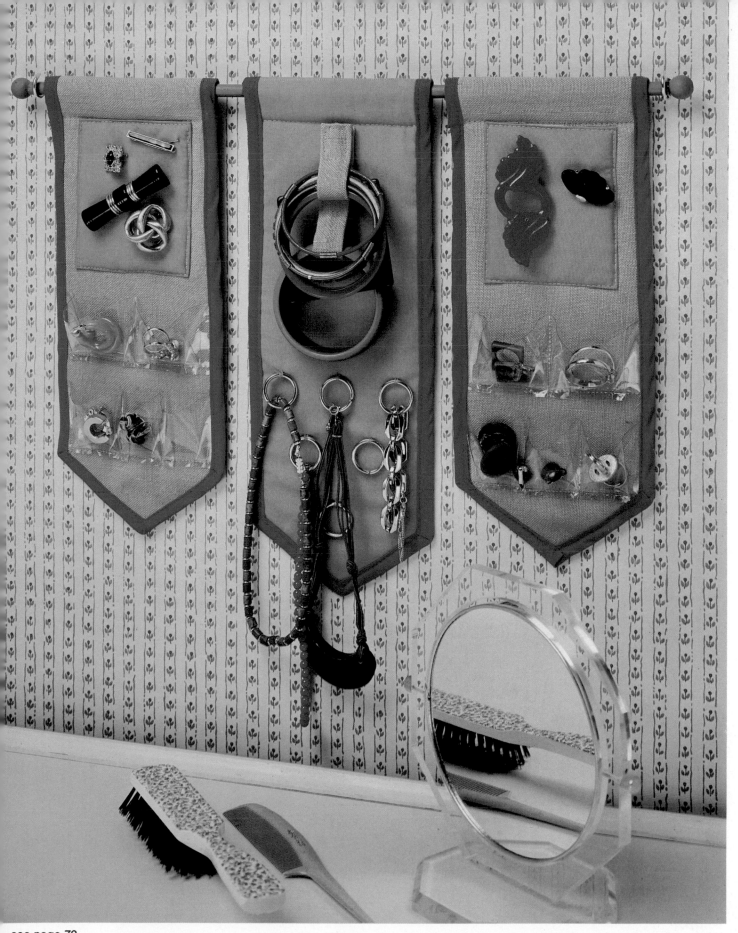

see page 72

see page 31

see page 146

see page 144

see page 112

see page 154

see page 55

see page 42

see page 60

see page 115

see page 19

see page 130

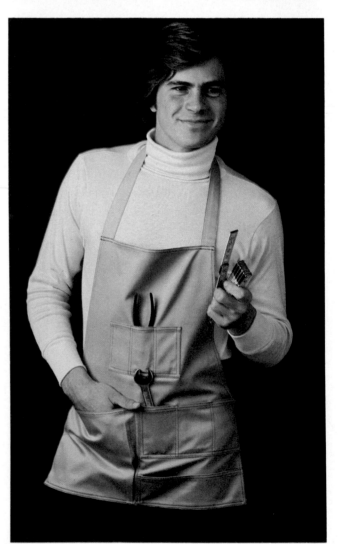

see page 27

see page 8

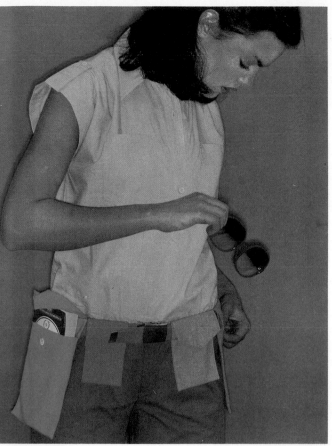

see page 151

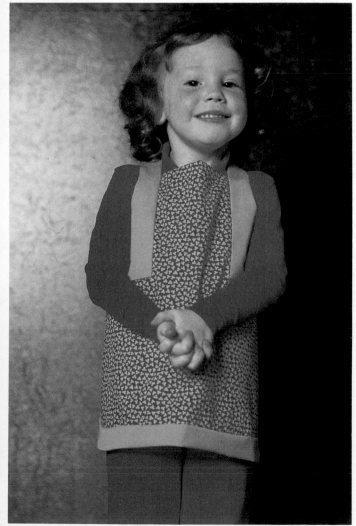

see page 121

see page 13   *see page 13*

see page 109

see page 40

see page 135

see page 137

see page 24

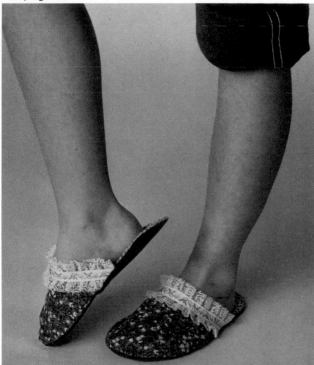

see page 99

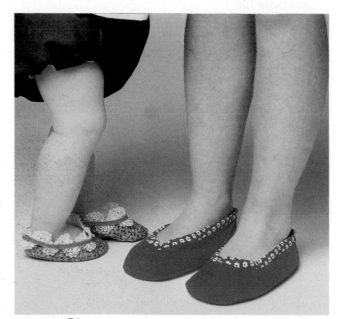

see page 51

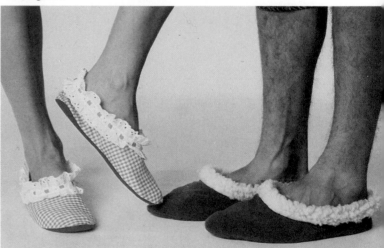

see page 24   *see page 51*

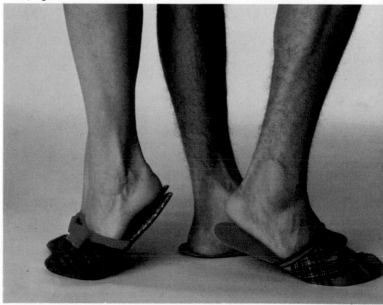

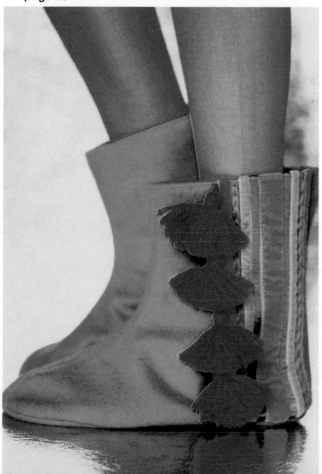

see page 57,

FOXY WALL HANGING

SIZE: 31" x 68".

MATERIALS: 1⅜ yards 54"-wide camel-colored upholstery velvet for background; ⅝ yard 45"-wide rust broadcloth for foxes; ⅜ yard 45"-wide white satin for fox details; ¼ yard 45"-wide charcoal suedelike cloth for top and bottom bands and fox features; ⅝ yard each chartreuse broadcloth and moss-green textured cotton for grass; matching sewing threads; 2½ yards 18"-wide iron-on bonding mesh; 5½ yards 1"-diameter upholstery cording for border; 1 yard tan broadcloth to cover cording; 33" x 70" piece 1"-thick quilt batting; 2 yards 36"-wide muslin (or a sheet) for backing; 6' of ½" x 1" pine lattice for heading.

BACKGROUND: From velvet, cut three 16" x 23" center panels and two 11½" x 23" end panels. Enlarge patterns (see How to Enlarge Patterns, page 6). Cut out rust fox all in one piece and white and charcoal details; do not add seam allowance.

Cut pieces of iron-on bonding mesh to match white and charcoal details. Bond details to fox with mesh. Machine-appliqué pieces with close zigzag stitch; pin fox to panel.

Cut out 2 more foxes, reversing one. Repeat procedure for bonding and appliquéing. Pin reversed fox to another panel, stitching right eyes on face. Pin third fox on remaining panel, stitching left eyes on face.

TALL GRASS: Following pattern, cut out grass pieces for right panel (do not add seam allowance). Reverse pattern and cut out grass pieces for left panel. Bond to panels with iron-on mesh and machine-appliqué with zigzag stitch, leaving ½" at side and lower edges free for seam allowance.

JOINING: With right sides facing, following photograph, stitch panels together, making ½" seams. From charcoal, cut two 3"-wide bands the length of hanging, piecing where necessary. Pin to top and bottom of panels, lapping raw charcoal edge over seam allowance on panels.

PADDING: Cut muslin (or sheet) same size as quilt batting. Center and baste batting and backing to back of hanging. Zigzag-stitch around each fox and around detail lines (eyes, along nose lines, front legs and tail) but not around white and charcoal details. Also stitch along seams between panels and along pinned bands. Trim backing and batting to edge of hanging.

BORDER: Cut 4"-wide *bias* strips of tan fabric, piecing them diagonally, to get 5½-yard length. Fold strip over cord and stitch close to cord. With raw edges matching, pin, then stitch cord around right side of hanging but do not stitch through backing fabric; round corners as shown. Match ends and hand-sew neatly. Clip corners on hanging to match rounded border. Turn under edges of backing and blindstitch to cord seam line.

HEADING: From tan fabric, cut three 2″ x 6″ strips for loops. Fold in half lengthwise, turn in ¼″ edges, and topstitch. Fold in half to form loops; sew a loop to each end of hanging and one to center, all three on wrong side near top but hidden from front view. Cut pine to fit and slide through loops. Hammer nails part way into wall and rest lattice on them. (For plaster or plasterboard walls, use screws set into anchors so that the shafts protrude enough to rest lattice on them.)

tasseled slipper Boots

Feet that have been skiing, skating, or shopping will feel pampered and pretty in these soft slippers. They're made of two thicknesses of felt to give body, and they have gay, folk-costume trimming.

Instructions on following pages >

TASSELED SLIPPER BOOTS

SIZE: Small (5–6) [medium (7–8), large (9–10)].

MATERIALS: 1¼ yards 36"-wide felt; 1 yard each ¼"-wide orange velvet, gold velvet, and blue satin ribbon; ½ yard ¾"-wide pink velvet ribbon; Persian-type crewel yarn, 1 (30-yard) skein medium-green and 8 skeins red; matching sewing thread; cardboard.

Note: Soles can be cut from vinyl or leather with fake fur inside, if desired.

Enlarge patterns for sides and sole to correct size (see How to Enlarge Patterns, page 6). Using patterns, cut four sides and two soles for each slipper, adding ½" seam allowance all around. (Each slipper has two thicknesses of felt for body.)

With right sides facing, pin sides of slipper together down front seam; stitch. Clip curved seam and press open. Topstitch along both sides of front seam. Fold over top edge as indicated by dotted line on pattern; topstitch. Following photograph, pin ribbons on outside of slipper; topstitch. Work a single row of chain stitches (see diagram, page 7) between orange and gold ribbons as in photograph, using 3 strands of green crewel yarn.

Temporarily baste two soles together for each foot. Beginning at toe, stitch assembled upper slipper along one side to heel. Repeat for remaining side, starting at toe. Leaving slipper wrong side out, stitch back seam two thirds of the way to top edge. Fold over and finish slit edges of back seam with two rows of machine stitching. Turn slipper to right side; remove basting stitches.

To make tassels cut a 2"-wide cardboard strip. Wind red crewel yarn around strip about 50 times. Slip bundle off strip and bind one end with 8 or 10 windings of a strand of yarn; knot to hold. Cut opposite ends to form tassel; trim ends even. Make 8 tassels. Tack 4 tassels, as in photograph, near ribbon appliqué toward front seam of each slipper.

Patterns to Enlarge for Tasseled Slipper Boots

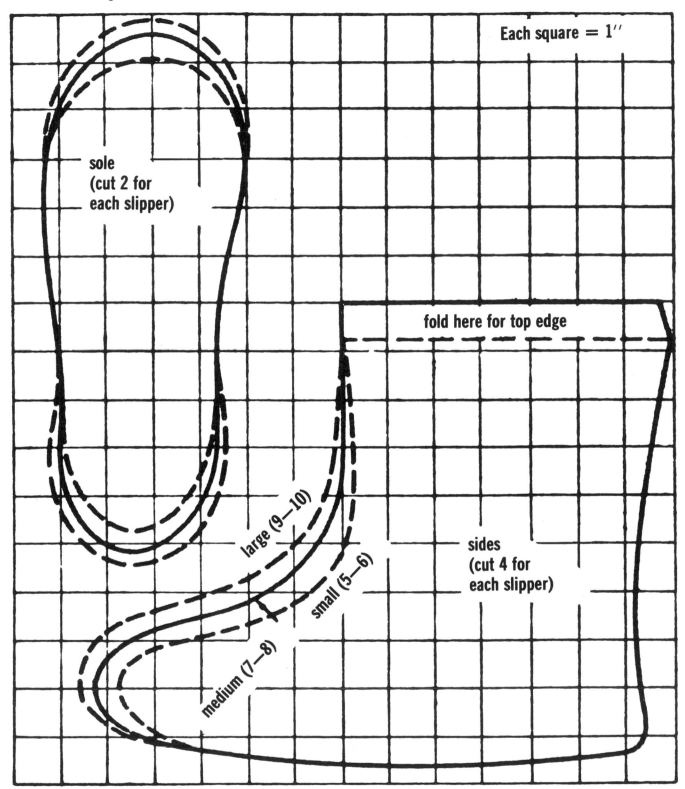

Each square = 1″

sole
(cut 2 for
each slipper)

fold here for top edge

sides
(cut 4 for
each slipper)

large (9—10)

small (5—6)

medium (7—8)

Stand-up Boy Doll

Like a good friend, he's comfortable to be around. Cotton-covered thick foam makes his body pillowy. He stands alone, more than 2 feet tall.

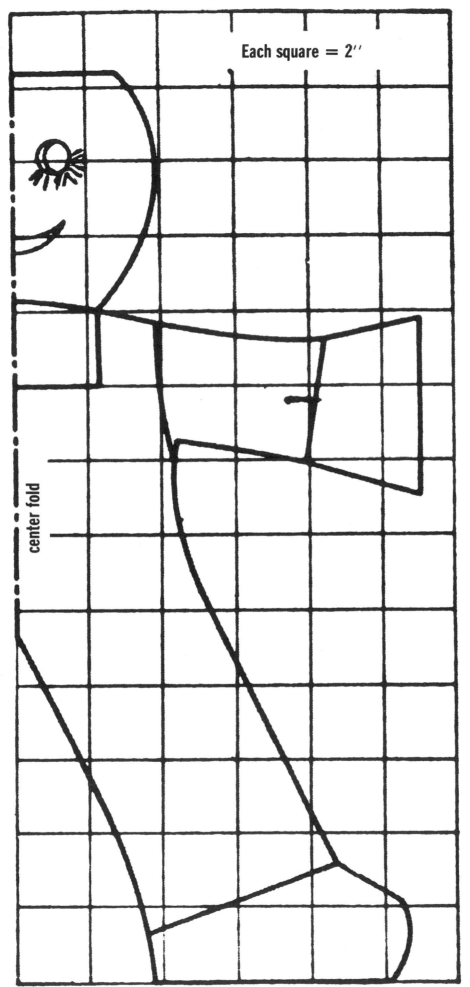

Each square = 2"

center fold

STAND-UP BOY DOLL

SIZE: 26″ tall.

MATERIALS: 36″-wide cotton fabric, 1 yard bright blue, ¾ yard orange, and ½ yard brown; ⅔ yard 36″-wide unbleached muslin; 22½″ x 26″ piece 4″-thick polyurethane foam; scraps orange, blue, and gold embroidery floss; matching sewing thread.

Enlarge pattern for doll, (see How to Enlarge Patterns, page 6). Cut out pattern and trace on foam with pencil. To cut foam, use a serrated bread knife or hacksaw blade.

The doll's head and hands are covered with unbleached muslin, the body with an orange shirt and blue overalls, and the feet with brown shoes. Use pattern for flat shapes and front and back pieces and cut side pieces to fit by taking measurements of the doll. Beginning with head, cut front and back pieces and a continuous strip going all the way around head; add ½″ all around for seams and extend bottom edges 3″ to fit securely under neck of shirt.

Transfer facial features to one rounded piece and fill in mouth, iris of eyes, and single star with satin stitch (see diagram, page 7). Use outline stitch around eyes and for eyelashes. To assemble head, pin long edge of side strip around front, right sides together; stitch. Add back piece and stitch. Turn right side out and slip over head of doll.

Cut front and back pieces for each hand, adding ½″ for seams and 2″ to tuck under wrist edge of shirt. Also cut side strip to go around side edges of hands with ½″ seam allowance on each side. With right sides together, pin front around side piece; stitch. Add back piece and stitch. Turn right side out and slip over hands.

From orange fabric cut front and back pieces for shirt, adding ½″ seam allowance and 3″ at bottom edge to tuck under overalls. Also cut two side pieces for each sleeve to cover top and underarm area with ½″ seam allowance on each side. With right sides together, pin top and underarm pieces to front piece; stitch. Slip shirt front on doll, wrapping sleeves around arms. Turning under raw edges, pin back piece in place. Neatly whipstitch seam together. Finish raw edges at neck and wrist.

From blue fabric cut front and back pieces for overalls, adding ½″ all around for seams and finishing. Also cut side pieces with ½″ seam allowance on each side for outside of both legs and for inside of both legs. Cut two strips for shoulder piece of overall straps. With right sides together, pin front to all side pieces; stitch. Slip front on doll;

wrap pants legs around each leg. Turning under raw edges, pin back piece in place. Neatly whipstitch seams together. Add shoulder pieces for straps. Turn under and hem raw neck, and arm edges.

From brown fabric cut front and back pieces of foot for shoes. Also cut a continuous strip to cover top of foot, toe, bottom, and heel with ½'' seam allowance on each side. With right sides together, pin front to strip; stitch. Add back and stitch. Turn shoes to right side and slip on feet. Push raw edges of shoes under leg edge of overalls. Turn under and hem leg edges.

Patchwork Place Mat

Couldn't be easier: you arrange calico scraps in this simple patchwork design, machine-topstitch the trapezoid shapes together, and bind the edge. You'll have long-lasting, good-looking results.

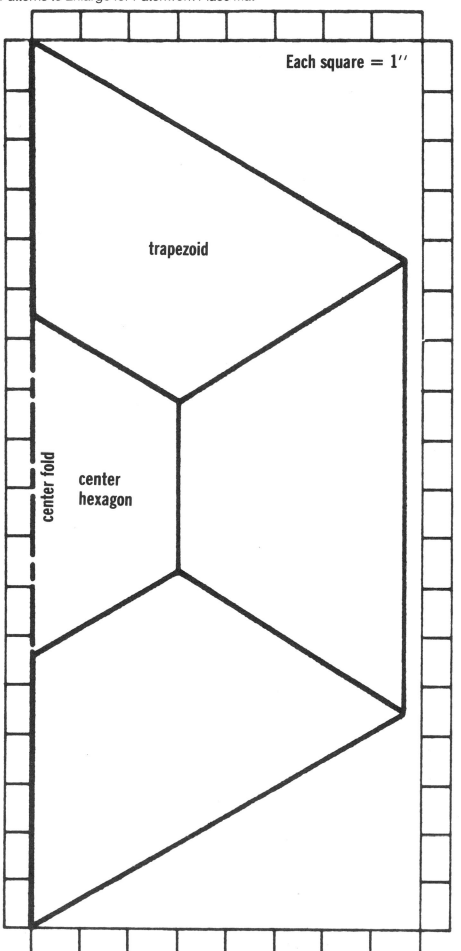

Each square = 1''

trapezoid

center fold

center
hexagon

PATCHWORK PLACE MAT

SIZE: 16½" from side to side.

MATERIALS: ½ yard calico for foundation; ⅜ yard of another calico for center section and edging; ¼ yard each of 2 contrasting calicoes for trapezoid segments; matching sewing thread.

Enlarge pattern (see How to Enlarge Patterns, page 6). Following outer edges of pattern, cut large hexagon from calico for foundation, adding ½" seam allowance. Cut 1 trapezoid pattern piece. Adding ½" seam allowance, cut out 2 trapezoid segments each from 2 contrasting calicoes. Press under seam allowance on slanting edges of each piece. Following photograph, pin, then baste trapezoids on right side of foundation. The 2 remaining pieces are foundation calico. Topstitch slanting edges of each piece.

Cut center hexagon pattern piece. Adding ½" seam allowance, cut from calico. Press under seam allowance, center on mat, and topstitch.

Cut 3½"-wide edging long enough to go around all sides plus 6" to allow for corners and overlap at joining. If necessary, piece edging to obtain required lengths. Fold in and press ¼" to ½" on both long edges of binding strip. Fold strip in half lengthwise so that folds meet at inside along one edge (like bias tape).

Apply to edges by slipping strip over edge of mat. Miter all corners and fold under ½" at end to overlap beginning of strip. Machine-topstitch through both folds encasing edge of mat.

Alternate method for odd shapes is to place one fold on top edge of mat, then sew on by hand through inside of that fold or machine-topstitch. Wrap other fold to the back and hand-stitch in place.

Use spray starch to add body to soft fabrics. Spray Scotchgard on untreated fabrics to help retard stains.

Fitted Evening Bag

Made of a quarter-yard of metallic fabric with black braid shoulder straps, it's zippered around three edges. Inside: a flap pocket with a snag-loop fastener, tiny mirror, and elastic bands to secure your comb, make-up pencils, and hanky.

Instructions on following pages ▶

FITTED EVENING BAG

SIZE: 5½″ x 7″ folded.

MATERIALS: ¼ yard each metallic fabric, nonwoven fusible interfacing, and cerise lining fabric; 16″ black zipper; matching sewing thread; ½ yard ½″-wide black elastic; 3 yards black braid; ½″-diameter Velcro spot fastener; 1½″-diameter round mirror; white glue.

Enlarge pattern (see How to Enlarge Patterns, page 6). Cut 1 bag piece each from metallic fabric, interfacing, and lining fabric, and 1 inside pocket piece each from metallic and lining fabric (½″ seam allowance is already included on all pattern pieces).

Cut seam allowance from interfacing pieces. Iron pocket and bag interfacing to wrong side of matching metallic fabric pieces. Turn under seam allowance of metallic fabric and baste.

Unzip zipper. With right sides facing you, start at fold line (broken line on pattern, bottom, left) and pin half of zipper around half of bag, and other half of zipper around other half of bag, so when bag is folded zipper will close. Baste and topstitch zipper around edges of metallic bag. Set aside.

To make inside pocket, with right sides facing, stitch edges of 2 pocket pieces together, leaving 2″ opening for turning. Trim seams, turn, and sew opening closed. Sew one section of Velcro fastener below point on flap. Fold along fold line (center broken line on pattern) and mark corresponding spot on pocket for other section of fastener. Sew fastener at marked spot.

Fold pocket with lining fabric on inside and pin side edges together. Baste pockets to one side of bag lining fabric (see pattern for placement). Topstitch pockets along 3 edges, leaving edge toward end of bag open; then topstich across center of piece to create 2 pockets. Glue mirror to one pocket.

Following diagram, pin and sew ends of 2 pieces of black elastic across other side of lining. Ease elastic to fit around makeup pencils and stitch in place.

Turn seam allowance of lining to inside and invisibly sew to wrong side of metallic bag.

To form shoulder straps, start at dot 1 on diagram and tack braid at each numbered dot on *metallic side* of bag, leaving 38″ of braid free for straps between 2 and 3 and 6 and 7. Cut off excess, then sew ends together.

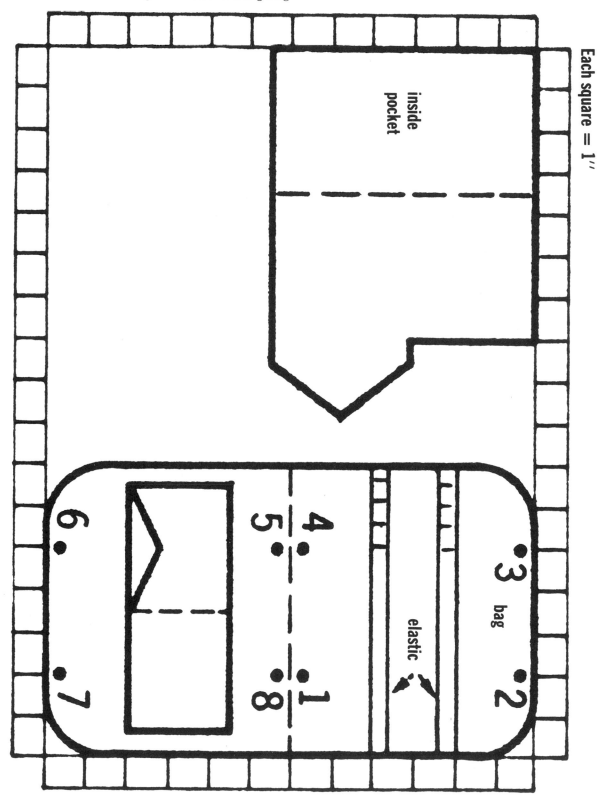

Each square = 1″

inside
pocket

6.

7.

5. 4.

8. 1.

3. bag

elastic

2.

Red-nosed Reindeer

Corduroy, various calico patterns, and a pompon tail make a dazzling turn-out for Santa's most beloved sled-puller. If he's intended for a child under three, substitute felt or embroidered decorations for the bells on his collar.

Patterns to Enlarge for Red-nosed Reindeer

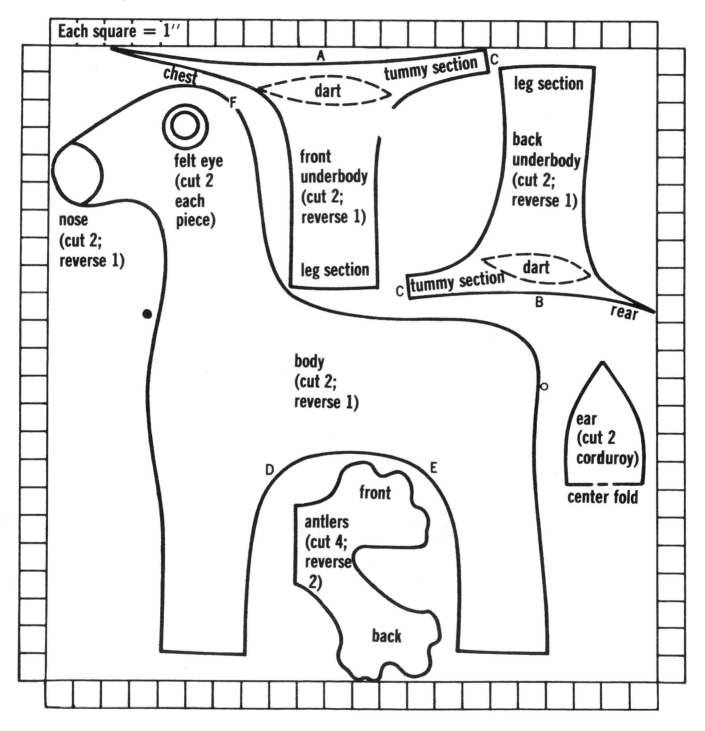

Each square = 1"

A
chest
tummy section
C
dart
leg section
F
felt eye
(cut 2
each
piece)
back
underbody
(cut 2;
reverse 1)
front
underbody
(cut 2;
reverse 1)
nose
(cut 2;
reverse 1)
leg section
C tummy section
dart
B
rear
body
(cut 2;
reverse 1)
ear
(cut 2
corduroy)
D
E
center fold
front
antlers
(cut 4;
reverse
2)
back

RED-NOSED REINDEER

SIZE: About 25" tall including antlers.

MATERIALS: ⅝-yard 45"-wide green corduroy for body; 36"-wide cotton-blend printed fabrics as follows: ⅝ yard red-dotted white fabric for underbody (includes inner legs), scraps white-dotted red fabric for nose, ¼ yard yellow calico for antlers; scraps of felt as follows: black and white for eyes, yellow and white for collar; 1 ounce white knitting-worsted-weight yarn or bulky yarn for tail; ¾ yard red rickrack; 6 jingle bells (not advisable for very small child's toy); polyester-fiberfill stuffing; matching sewing thread; white glue.

PATTERNS: Enlarge pattern (see How to Enlarge Patterns, page 6). Cut out fabric pieces, adding ½" to all edges for seam allowance (do not add to felt eyes).

ASSEMBLING: Underbody: Stitch darts in underbody pieces. With right sides facing, matching points on chest, stitch shaped edges (A) of front underbodies together. Matching points on rear, stitch shaped edges (B) of back underbodies together. Join front and back underbodies at C (seams crosses center of tummy).

Body: Appliqué dotted nose pieces to corduroy body pieces. Stitch body pieces together from dot on chest, around head, along back, to circle on rear. Stitch underbody to 1 body piece, matching chest point on front underbody to dot and rear point on back underbody to circle, stitching around front leg, along tummy, and around hind leg. Stitch free edge of underbody to other body piece, leaving tummy from D to E open for turning. Clip seam allowance at curves. Turn and stuff firmly so reindeer stands.

Ears: Stitch ear pieces together, leaving 3" open on 1 side. Turn and pad pointed ends lightly. Tie ear unit tight at center to pleat; sew tied center to head at F.

Antlers and Eyes: Stitch matching halves of antlers together, leaving straight ends open. Turn and stuff firmly; sew openings closed. Following photograph, hold antlers together near base so they fan out slightly; sew where they touch. Sew to head in front of ears. Glue eyes to head.

Tail: For pompon, wrap yarn around 4"-wide piece of cardboard about 60 to 80 times, depending on thickness of yarn. Cut yarn along 1 edge of cardboard and tie strands together tight at center. Trim pompon and sew to rear.

Collar: From felt, cut 2"-wide yellow band and ¾"-wide white band to fit around neck. Topstitch white band along center of yellow band. Cut 2 strips rickrack to fit along edges of collar and stitch in place. Sew bells around white band. Turn in ends of collar and sew around neck, shaping to fit slant of back neck.

Peas-in-Pod Toy

Three wee happy peas snap into a zippered pod—and teach little fingers how to snap and zip. A half yard of fabric does it, and if your scrap bag doesn't yield a pea-green remnant, create a "hybrid" vegetable with whatever you have available.

Instructions on following pages ⟩

PEAS-IN-POD TOY

SIZE: 6″ x 18″.

MATERIALS: ½ yard 45″-wide green cotton fabric; green sewing thread; scraps of black iron-on tape; 3 large snaps; 16″ zipper; polyester-fiberfill stuffing.

Transfer pattern to tracing paper and cut out, adding ½″ seam allowance all around. Cut out 4 full pod pieces (cut one end of pod following solid line and other end following broken lines).

With right sides facing, stitch pairs of pod pieces together along curved lower edge. Trim and clip seams. With wrong sides facing, insert 1 pod section in other. Turn in raw top edges and baste. Insert zipper at top edge. Sew seams at ends of pods.

Cut six 5½″-diameter fabric circles. Stitch pairs together, leaving 2″ opening. Trim and clip seams; turn. Blindstitch opening. Cut features from black tape (see photograph) and iron to peas. Stuff. Sew snaps to bottoms of peas and to bottom seam on inside of pod.

Full-size Patterns for Peas-in-Pod Toy

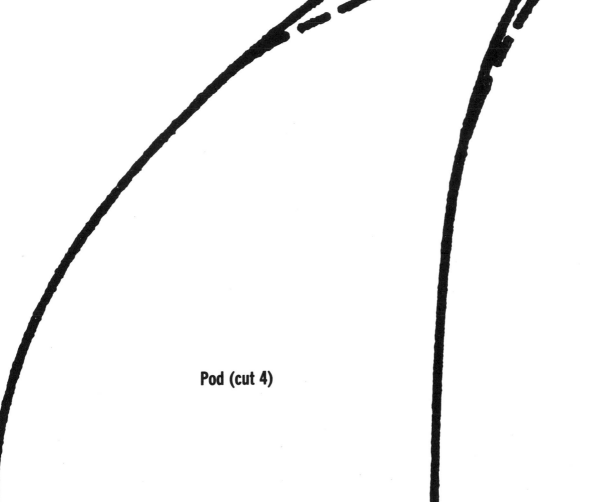

Pod (cut 4)

center fold

SILLY FACE-MAKERS

They smile, they frown; they'll make youngsters smile too. Their eyes, noses, mouths, and clumps of yarn hair are all interchangeable. It's a cinch for small fry to switch the features on these huggable funny fellows because each part is backed with a piece of snag-loop fastening tape that adheres to the terry cloth.

Patterns to Enlarge for Silly Face-makers

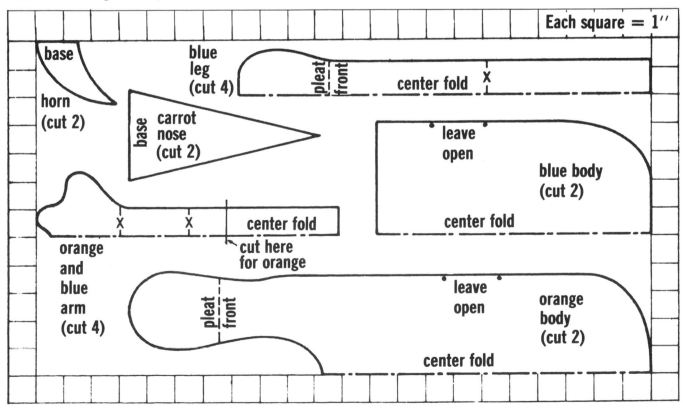

Each square = 1"

base

blue leg (cut 4)

pleat front

center fold X

horn (cut 2)

base carrot nose (cut 2)

leave open

blue body (cut 2)

center fold

orange and blue arm (cut 4)

X   X   center fold

cut here for orange

leave open

orange body (cut 2)

pleat front

center fold

center fold

SILLY FACE-MAKERS

SIZES: Orange is 15" tall, blue is 20" tall.

MATERIALS: 45"-wide looped (unsheared) terry cloth, ⅝ yard orange or ½ yard blue; scraps of felt in assorted colors; pieces of snag-loop fastening tape such as Velcro (hooked section only as tape will stick to terry cloth); cardboard; bulky gift-wrap yarn; fabric glue; polyester-fiberfill stuffing; matching sewing thread.

PATTERNS: Enlarge patterns (see How to Enlarge Patterns, page 6), and cut out, adding ½" seam allowance to all edges. **Note:** Cut orange arms shorter; add seam allowance to cut edge.

BODY: With right sides facing, stitch pairs of matching pieces together (bodies, arms, legs), leaving opening (bottom on blue) for turning. Turn and stuff. Baste closed tops of arms and legs. Insert arms in body between dots and blue legs in bottom of body. Topstitch (on blue, stitch right across bottom of body and across X lines on arms and legs; omit X lines for orange). Bend each foot forward at broken line, making pleat. Hand-sew pleat to form foot.

FEATURES: Hair: Cut yarn into 4" lengths. Tie 20 or 25 lengths together tightly around center to form shaggy pompon. Cut 1¼" square of matching felt and, pushing all cut ends of pompon upward, glue square to center bottom of pompon and fastening tape to other side of felt.

Eyes, Mouths, Cheeks: Following photograph, cut pieces of each feature from felt and glue together. Place each finished feature on cardboard, trace around it and cut out. Glue feature to cardboard; glue fastening tape to other side of cardboard.

Round Nose: Cut 4"-diameter felt circle. Sew running stitches around circle close to edge, pulling up to form pouch. Stuff firmly and sew pouch closed. Glue fastening tape over gathers.

Carrot Nose: Following pattern, cut nose from orange terry-cloth. Stitch pieces together, leaving base open. Turn and stuff. Cut 2"-diameter cardboard circle and insert in nose; pull terry over it and glue to form flat base. Glue fastening tape to base. Cut ¼"-wide strips of darker orange felt scraps and glue in rings around cone.

Horns: Following pattern, cut horns from felt. Stitch pairs together, leaving base open. Trim and clip seams; turn and stuff firmly. Cut two 1"-diameter cardboard circles; insert 1 in each horn and finish as for carrot nose.

Hat: You will need an empty 2"-long sewing thread spool for crown. Glue strip of red felt around spool and circle of felt to 1 end. For brim, cut 3"-diameter cardboard circle and cover both sides with felt. Glue crown to center of brim. Glue ⅜"-wide yellow felt strip around crown; glue fastening tape to bottom of brim.

Bow Tie: Cut 3½" x 16" strip yellow felt. Fold ¼ of length in from each end, overlapping ends at center. Wrap and glue (or sew) 1¾" x 5" felt strip around middle. Glue fastening tape to back of tie.

child's pinafore apron

A sweet, old-fashioned design with crossed straps in back that's all set for playtime over today's polyester blends. It calls for only a third-yard each of calico print and contrasting solid-color cotton fabric.

Instructions on following pages >

CHILD'S PINAFORE-APRON

SIZE: Fits ages 4–9.

MATERIALS: ⅓ yard each calico print and contrasting solid cotton fabric; matching sewing thread; small snaps.

Enlarge patterns for basic apron and contrasting trim (see How to Enlarge Patterns, page 6). Cut out paper patterns, adding ½" seam allowance all around and 1" at top edge of apron for fold-over hem. Cut out contrasting trim from solid fabric, extending strip for crossed shoulder straps to 17". Also cut two 1¾" x 17" strips from solid fabric for underside of straps. Cut out calico apron.

Fold over and stitch hem across top edge of apron; press. With right sides together, center separate strap pieces on straps extended from trim. Stitch along long sides and top edges, leaving bottom edge open. Turn straps and press. Turn up and hem single raw edge on straps.

With right sides facing you, place apron on top of trim, matching edges. Stitch contrasting trim around outer edge of apron. Trim and clip seam at curves. Fold trim to right side of calico apron and press. Turning under raw edges, slipstitch inner edge of trim to apron. Try on apron, crossing straps at back, and determine placement for snaps to fasten at top of side edges. Sew snaps in place.

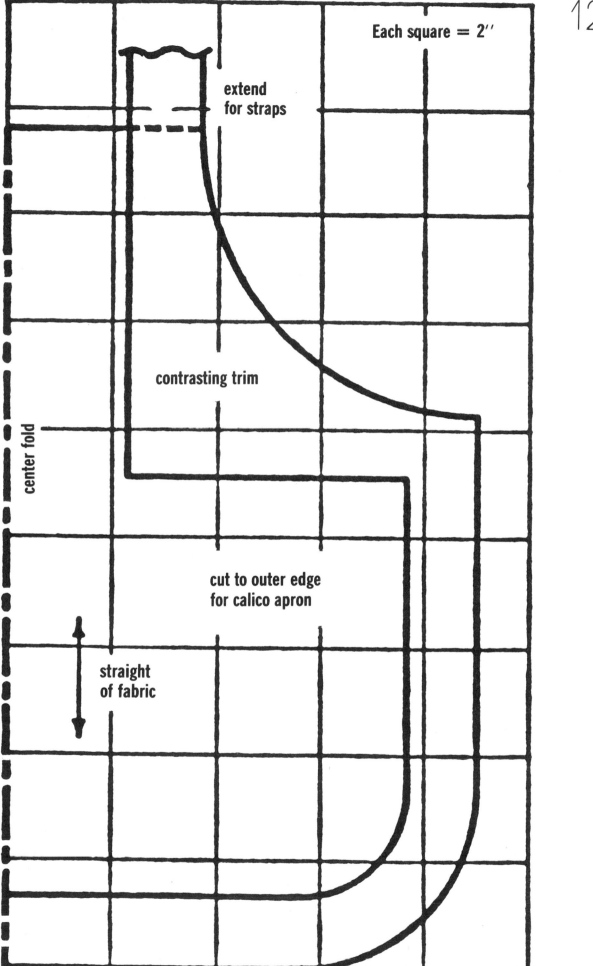

123

Each square = 2''

extend
for straps

contrasting trim

center fold

cut to outer edge
for calico apron

straight
of fabric

PATCHWORK SITTING DUCK

A colorful pillow as well as a good toy for younger children, Mama Duck has a slender neck and legs that are easy for tiny hands to grasp and carry around.

Patterns to Enlarge for Patchwork Sitting Duck

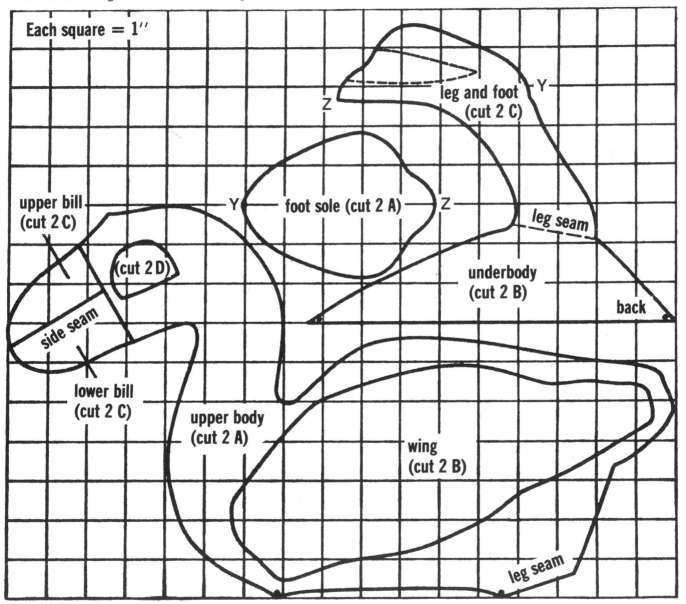

Each square = 1"

leg and foot
(cut 2 C)

Z

Y

foot sole (cut 2 A)

Y

Z

upper bill
(cut 2 C)

(cut 2 D)

leg seam

underbody
(cut 2 B)

back

side seam

lower bill
(cut 2 C)

upper body
(cut 2 A)

wing
(cut 2 B)

leg seam

PATCHWORK SITTING DUCK

SIZE: About 15″ long.

MATERIALS: 45″-wide cotton fabric, ½ yard each green print (A) and pink polka dot (B), ¼ yard orange-and-yellow print (C); scrap of pink print (D); polyester-fiberfill stuffing; matching sewing thread.

Enlarge patterns, (see How to Enlarge Patterns, page 6), and cut whole pattern (including leg and foot) for underbody and another pattern to dotted line for upper leg and foot. Cut remaining pattern pieces. Adding ¼″ seam allowance to wings and eyes and ½″ seams to all other edges, cut out fabric pieces indicated on patterns. Cut underbody with leg and foot from B; cut upper leg and foot only from C.

UPPER BODY: First Side: Press under raw edges of wing and eye. Topstitch to upper body. With right sides facing, stitch upper and lower bill pieces together at side seam. With right sides facing, stitch bill and C upper leg and foot to upper body.

Second Side: Work same as for first side. With right sides facing, stitch upper-body pieces together, leaving lower edge open between dots.

UNDERBODY: With right sides facing, seam straight edge of underbody pieces from dot to dot, leaving 3″ open at center (for turning when duck is completed).

With right sides facing, matching raw edges and dots, pin underbody between duck sides and pin upper and under leg pieces together, leaving feet open between Y and Z. With right sides facing, matching raw edges and Y's and Z's, pin sole between feet pieces. Stitch all seams. Clip curves; turn.

Stuff feet lightly. Topstitch along broken lines on pattern. Stuff remainder of duck firmly. Blindstitch opening closed.

SUNBONNET SUE PILLOW

Transfer the charming design to bleached muslin, then create a trapunto effect by lightly padding the bonnet, apron bow, arm, hand, flower, one foot, and corner motifs.

Instructions on following pages >

SUNBONNET SUE PILLOW

SIZE: Curved pillow measures about 12½" x 15".

MATERIALS: ½ yard 45"-wide bleached muslin; permanent felt-tipped laundry marker; matching sewing thread; 1 pound polyester-fiberfill stuffing; dressmaker's carbon.

Note: Practice using laundry marker on scrap muslin. Place newspaper or paper towel under muslin when marking to absorb extra ink.

From muslin cut 2 pieces 13½" x 16"; set one piece aside for back. Enlarge pattern, (see How to Enlarge Patterns, page 6). Place carbon face down on muslin; center pattern on top. With sharp pencil or stylus transfer complete design to muslin. Remove pattern and carbon. With laundry marker go over design on muslin.

When marks are dry, lightly pad bonnet, apron bow, arm, hand, flower, one foot, and corner motifs (X on diagram) for trapunto as follows: Cut piece of muslin ¼" larger all around than one trapunto area; place this piece on wrong side of marked muslin under area and, using matching thread and running stitch, sew together around outline of area, leaving small opening for stuffiing; stuff and sew closed.

With right sides facing, sew top and back pieces together by stitching 1" from curved border line and leaving 5" opening for stuffing. Turn and stuff. Blindstitch opening.

Dry-clean pillow to avoid fading.

center

Each space between dots = 1″

center

Bouncy Funnel Dolls

When a youngster twirls the dowel handle, the doll swishes merrily up and down. The bodies for mother, father, brother, and sister are funnels; heads are plastic-foam balls covered with flannel; hair is yarn; clothes are fabric scraps.

SIZE: About 18″ tall.

MATERIALS: For each parent: 5½″-diameter x 5½″-high aluminum or plastic funnel for body; 18″ of ⅜″-diameter dowel; 2″-diameter plastic-foam ball for head; 6½″ x 19″ pieces print cotton fabric, 1 each of 2 different prints. **For each child:** 3½″-diameter x 4″-high aluminum or plastic funnel for body; 18″ of ¼″-diameter dowel; 1½″-diameter plastic-foam ball for head; 5″ x 12½″ pieces print or plain cotton fabric, 1 each of 2 different kinds (or ribbed section of sock as shown on boy doll). **For all dolls:** Scraps of yarn for hair; scraps of skin-color flannel to cover heads; trimmings such as felt and fabric scraps, seam binding, ribbon, ruffled eyelet lace, and colored string; felt-tipped markers or crayons for features; white glue.

MOTHER: Push dowel into plastic-foam ball ½″ or so and glue in place; let dry. Cut flannel circle to cover ball and extend about 1″ onto dowel. Stretch tightly over ball, gathering with a few stitches around neck. Glue excess flannel to dowel.

Cut yarn into 10″ strands and spread thickly and evenly over top of head. For center part sew hair to flannel. Pull hair back and tie loosely with strand of yarn. Draw eyes, cheeks, and mouth with markers or crayons.

With right sides facing, stitch fabric rectangles (top and bottom garment pieces) together along one long edge, making ½″ seam. Fold in half crosswise and, for back seam, stitch ends together to form tube. Turn under 1 edge (neck) of top section ¾″ and stitch ½″ from fold; stitch again ⅛″ from last stitching line to form casing. Poke hole in center front of casing. Run 10″ length of colored string through casing, allowing ends to extend through hole. Slide garment on doll. Pull string tight around neck and tie in bow at front. Tack to neck.

Slide dowel into upturned funnel. Pull garment over funnel and glue seam (joining top and bottom sections) around top of funnel. Trim glue seam with eyelet lace ruffle and ribbon. Sew running stitches around bottom of garment and pull tight around spout. Glue excess to spout. Wrap tightly with strip of ribbon glued in place.

FATHER: Assemble as for Mother, making following changes: Cut 5½″ yarn lengths for hair. After sewing center part, cut a few front strands for bangs and glue remaining strands to head.

Turn under neck edge of garment ½″ and topstitch ¼″ from fold. Run 6″ string through seam, pull tight and tie, hiding knot inside. Cut white fabric collar and glue around neck. Tie ribbon strip to form bow tie and glue in place.

Trim seam around funnel with ¼''-wide ribbon or seam binding. Cut buckle from 1'' x 1¼'' piece of ribbon and glue in place.

GIRL: Assemble as for Mother, making following changes: Cut 9'' yarn lengths for hair. After sewing center part, braid hair in 2 pigtails and tie with yarn.

Run 6'' string through neck casing, pull tight and tie, hiding knot inside. Wrap length of yarn several times around outside of neck casing and tie in back.

Trim seam around funnel with ruffled eyelet lace.

BOY: Assemble as for Mother, making following changes: Cut 4'' yarn lengths for hair. Sew seam for side part and glue hair to head.

For garment top, instead of fabric use 6'' ribbed cuff cut from sock to simulate sweater. Fold cuff down 1¾'' and run basting thread around cuff 1'' from fold. For garment bottom use fabric rectangle and seam ends together to form tube. Stitch 1 edge of tube around basting line on knitted top; turn down cuff. Slide garment on doll, sew running stitches around neck and pull tight. Make a few stitches in neck to hold garment in place. Cut 1'' x 3½'' ribbed strip from other sock. Seam ends to form tube; slide tube over head and fold in half around neck to form turtleneck.

Cut hat from felt as follows: Cut 1¾''-diameter circle for top, ⅝''-wide strip to fit around circle for sides and ½'' x 1½'' half oval for peak. Sew ends of strip together to form ring; sew ring around circle. Sew straight edge of half oval to edge of cap.

TO PLAY WITH DOLLS: To make doll dance, twirl dowel quickly between fingers and thumb; funnel will bounce up and down and twist from side to side.

Quilt-square Pillow

The top is pieced from simple calico shapes and looks just like a quilt square. Primary-colored calicoes were chosen for a bright, cheerful look.

Instructions on following pages >

QUILT-SQUARE PILLOW

SIZE: 17" square.

MATERIALS: ½"-yard 45"-wide yellow calico, ¼ yard each red and blue calico; ½ yard muslin for lining; matching sewing thread; 17"-square foam pillow form or polyester-fiberfill stuffing; cardboard for patterns; graph paper.

PATTERNS: On graph paper mark off 7" square, 5" square, and 5" x 3½" x 3½" triangle. Cut out and trace on cardboard. Cut out cardboard patterns.

CUTTING: For front pattern, on wrong side of fabric trace one 7" yellow square, four 5" red squares, 4 red triangles, and 8 blue triangles (leave at least ½" between pieces). Cut out pieces, adding ¼" seam allowance to all edges. Also from yellow calico, cut four 1¾" x 18" strips for border and 18" square for pillow back.

STITCHING: Follow photograph for arrangement of pieces. With right sides facing, stitch 2 blue triangles to adjacent sides of each red square. Stitch a free edge on each blue triangle to yellow center square. Stitch 4 red triangles to remaining free edges of blue triangles to complete large square. Press seams to one side at each joining (do not press seams open). Stitch a border strip to each side of large square, mitering corners. With right sides facing, stitch patchwork front and back together with ½" seams, leaving 15" open on one side.

LINING: From muslin, cut two 18" squares. Stitch together with ½" seams, leaving 15" open on one side. Turn and insert pillow form or stuffing. Close opening. Slip pillow in patchwork case and blindstitch closed.

Posh Mini Totes

Perfect for evening and so quick and easy you'll be making them by the dozen—just a rectangle of velvet folded in half, lined with satin, elasticized at the top, and suspended on rattail-cord "necklaces" in contrasting colors.

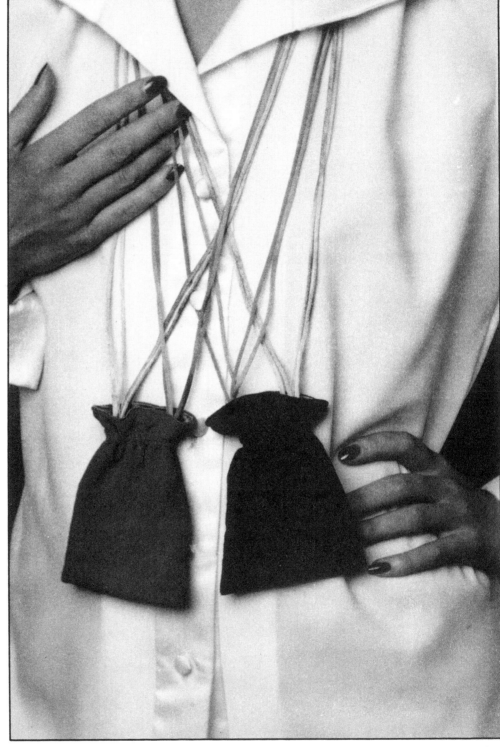

Instructions on following pages ›

POSH MINI TOTES

SIZE: Each tote measures 3½" x 5".

MATERIALS: For each tote: 4½" x 10½" piece each velvet and contrasting lining fabric (we used green velvet with pink satin lining and red velvet with aqua satin lining); 1 yard each ⅛"-diameter rattail in 4 different colors (we used red, orange, pink, and lavender); 5" piece ¼"-wide flat elastic; matching sewing thread.

Fold velvet rectangle in half crosswise wrong side out. Stitch ½" side seams. Trim seams; turn. Stitch lining rectangle in same manner.

Insert lining in velvet pouch, wrong sides facing. Turn raw (top) edges in ¼" and topstitch. For casing, stitch ¾" and 1¼" from top edge. Open 1 side seam of casing; insert elastic and sew ends together. Close opening.

Fold each length of rattail in half. Stitch ends of 2 lengths to lining at each side seam on casing.

CARRY-ALL BARREL BAG

Measuring 21" long, 10" in diameter and having a pocket at each end, it's truly a roomy tote. We used denim covered with assorted fabric scraps for patches, lined it with wide-wale corduroy, and finished the ends with tassels.

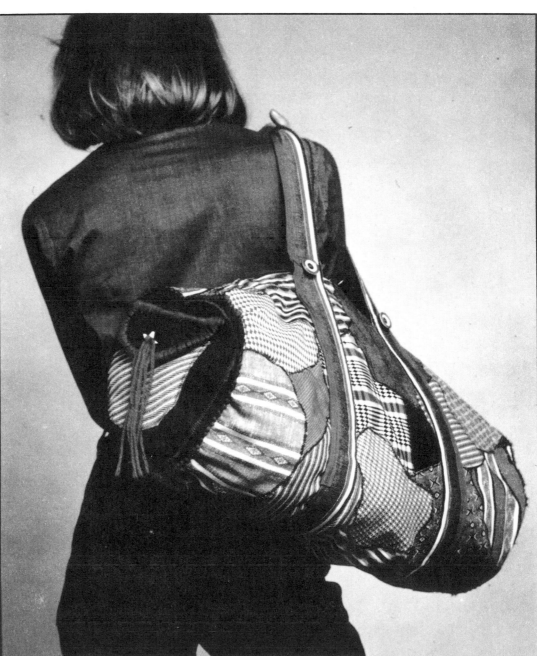

Instructions on following pages ❯

CARRY-ALL BARREL BAG

SIZE: 21″ long, 10″ in diameter.

MATERIALS: 1 yard 45″-wide blue denim; ⅝ yard 45″-wide wide-wale corduroy for lining; assorted fabric scraps for patches (we used mostly woven denim in blues, reds, and white); small amount red knitting worsted; tapestry needle; 14″ heavy-duty zipper; 6 decorative buttons; 3½ yards each 1″-wide red grosgrain ribbon and ⅝″-wide red, white, and blue grosgrain ribbon; matching sewing thread.

CUTTING: For tube backing, cut one 22″ x 34″ piece each for denim and corduroy, with ribs on corduroy running parallel to 22″ measurement. For ends cut two 11″ circles each from denim and corduroy. For handles cut 4½″-wide denim strips and piece into one 110″-long length. For end pockets cut two 5″ squares from fabric scraps. Round 2 corners on each for lower edge. For pocket flaps cut two 4½″-diameter denim circles. Cut circles in half for 4 flap pieces. Pin pairs together, right sides out, for 2 flaps.

PATCH PIECING: Cut irregular shapes from fabric scraps to cover denim tube piece, overlapping shapes slightly. Pin in place. Topstitch with machine zigzag attachment around all raw edges except outer edges of piece. Trim to match edges of tube.

ASSEMBLING: With right sides facing, stitch corduroy and denim tube pieces together along 34″ edges, making ½″ seams. Turn.

Turn under ½″ at top edge of pockets and topstitch. Zigzag-stitch pockets to right side of denim circles. Zigzag-stitch a decorative ring in red around circles 1″ in from edge. With yarn and tapestry needle, whipstitch closely around edges of pocket flaps. Sew flaps in place. With right sides facing, stitch pairs of denim and corduroy circles together to make 2 ends, leaving opening on each for turning. Turn and blindstitch opening.

With right sides of pieces facing out and starting at center of a seamed edge on tube piece, pin edge halfway around a circle, allowing excess to extend beyond circle. Then pin other half of same tube edge around remainder of circle, allowing excess to extend. Pin opposite seamed edge around other circle in same manner. Turn in raw edges of excess and baste.

With yarn and tapestry needle, whipstitch circles to tube. Insert zipper in center of basted opening. Whipstitch openings at ends of zipper and cover with ribbon strips.

STRAPS: Fold denim strap in half lengthwise, right side out.

Fold 1″-wide ribbon over raw edges and topstitch. Topstitch striped ribbon along one side of opposite folded edge (right side of strap). Seam ends of strap to form large ring. Place ring on table, wrong side up, and arrange it into an oval. Place tote across center of oval, lift ends of oval for handles. Pin straps in place, then topstitch.

Sew button to each pocket flap and attach 6″-long yarn tassel as shown in photograph. Sew a button to base of each handle.

Soft Eyeglasses Case

No pattern, no seams—all you do is cut rectangles from small pieces of felt with pinking shears, topstitch them together and glue on a big circle like a notary seal.

SIZE: 4¼'' x 7½''.

MATERIALS: 4¼'' x 7'' turquoise felt; 4¼'' x 10'' red felt; scrap of green felt; red sewing thread; fabric glue; pinking shears.

Pink ends of red rectangle. Cut 2¼'' circle from green felt with pinking shears. Match sides and one end of rectangles and stitch together twice, ⅛'' and ¼'' from edge. Fold red flap down; topstitch along fold. Glue circle to flap.

BEDSIDE CADDY POCKET

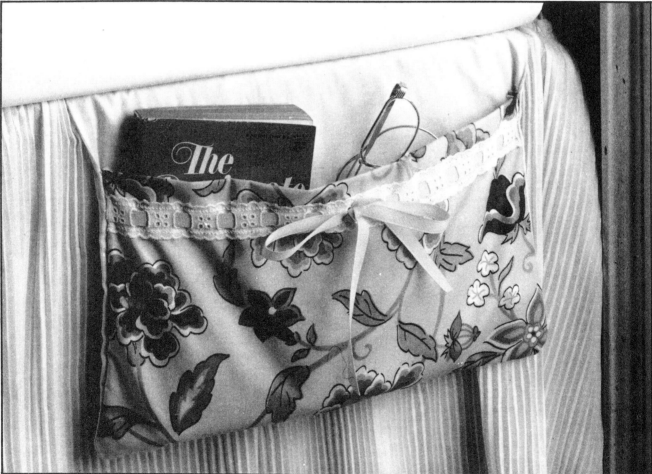

Cleverly constructed with a piece of cardboard to stiffen the end that slips under the mattress, this convenient accessory holds eyeglasses, reading material, and whatnot, and even has a separate matching case for a pocket-size pack of tissues.

SIZE: Pocket measures about 12½″ x 17½″, including part that goes under mattress. Tissue holder measures 3″ x 5″ (holds pocket tissue package).

MATERIALS: For Both Items: ½ yard 45″-wide white cotton fabric; ¼ yard 45″ floral-print chintz; 13½″ piece cotton eyelet lace; 1 yard ⅜″-wide grosgrain ribbon to match chintz; 12″ piece 1″-wide bias tape to match chintz; 12″ piece 1″-wide pregathered eyelet lace; 9″ x 12½″ piece cardboard.

Note: Sew ½″ seams.

BED POCKET: Cut 8″ x 13 ½″ piece each chintz and white fabric (lining). Cut ribbon in half and weave through eyelet lace so that one end of each piece extends at center of lace. Tack other ends to lace. Sew lace and ribbon strip to right side of chintz 1″ from one long edge (top).Tie bow with free ends of ribbon.With right sides facing, sew lining to chintz along top edge. Turn lining to wrong side of chintz.

Cut two 13½″ x 18½″ pieces white fabric and, with right sides facing, sew together across long edges to form tube. Turn.

With right sides facing, place raw long edge of chintz pocket piece at one end of tube. Seam along lower and side edges, stitching close to seam edges of tube.

Turn open end of tube under ½″ and hem. Slide cardboard in open end (this part goes under mattress).

TISSUE HOLDER: Cut 6″ x 6¾″ piece chintz; cut two 6″ lengths each of pregathered lace and bias tape.

Sew a piece of pregathered lace ¼″ from each 6″ edge of chintz on right side of fabric. Fold bias tape over same edges, covering previous stitching, and sew in place.

With right sides facing, fold rectangle in thirds so that trimmed edges meet at center. Seam raw ends. Turn right side out. Insert in bed pocket.

Soft Nursery Blocks

They're a good size—three-inch cubes—and soft for little fingers to play with. Foam rubber is covered with fabric scraps; numbers and letters are colorful iron-on fabric.

MATERIALS: ¼ yard 12″-wide, 3″-thick foam rubber (enough for 12 blocks); assorted scraps of fabric; fusible fabric (we used Bondex); matching sewing thread.

Cut foam rubber into 3″ squares with a serrated bread knife or hacksaw. For each block, cut six 4″ squares of fabric (½″ seam allowance included). Cut 2 letters or numbers from fusible fabric and iron on 2 squares. Using 1 fabric square with letter or number as base, with right sides facing, stitch 1 square to each side of base. Stitch sides of squares to form box; turn right side out. Insert foam. Turn under raw edges of remaining square (with letter or number); blind-stitch to block.

Patchwork Flowerpots

No sewing is required, so these are great for a child to make (and give as gifts). Assemble any-size plastic flowerpots, an assortment of fabric scraps, pinking shears, and white glue, and the production line is set for action.

MATERIALS: Any size plastic flowerpot; assorted fabric scraps; white glue; pinking shears; small paintbrush.

Cut fabric into strips, squares, or any other desired shapes with pinking shears. In plastic bowl dilute 2 parts glue with 1 part water. Dip fabric in glue, then apply to pot. Overlap all fabric pieces to cover outside of pot completely, folding fabric over top edge to cover inside of rim. When dry, brush on glaze of equal parts glue and water.

Yo-yo Place Mat

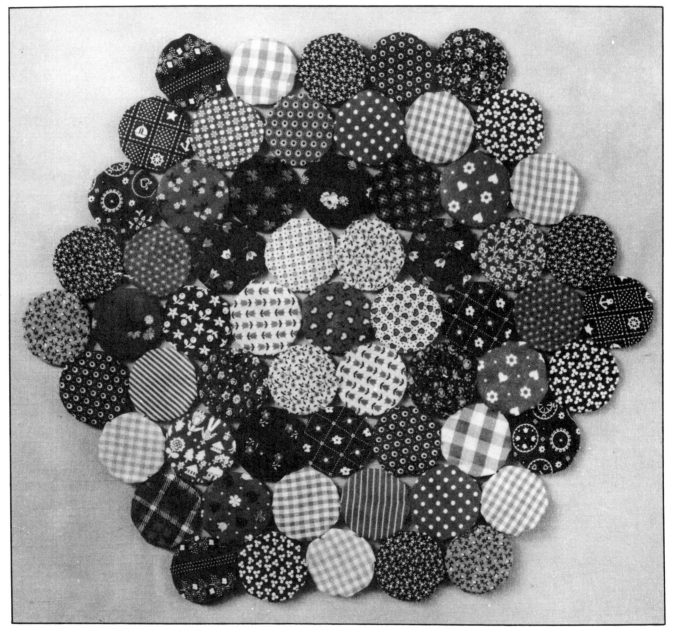

A yo-yo is a circle of fabric shirred tightly to form a small "mob cap." You'll need 61 of them, made from cotton scraps and sewn together, for this hexagon mat.

SIZE: 19" hexagon, measured from point to opposite point.

MATERIALS: An assortment of 61 cotton-fabric scraps (at least 5" square) in coordinated prints (see note below); nylon sewing thread; compass.

Note: We used prints with red, blue, and yellow backgrounds. To make mat similar to ours, you will need 36 scraps of blue print, 19 scraps of red, and 6 scraps of yellow.

TO MAKE YO-YO: With compass, mark 5"-diameter circle on right side of each fabric scrap for cutting line. Then, mark another circle ¼" inside first on each scrap for hemline. Cut out circles. Clip ¼" apart around circumference of circles almost to hemline so that hem allowance will lie flat when folded.

Fold hem to inside along hemline and, using sewing needle and nylon thread, sew small running stitches around circle; pull up to gather very tightly so that circle forms shape of small "mob cap." Fasten securely. Press flat.

TO ASSEMBLE: Follow photograph to arrange yo-yos with sides touching. Sew together where they touch.

Use spray starch to add body to soft fabrics. Spray Scotchgard on untreated fabrics to help retard stains.

POCKET-PACKING BELT

Four pockets in four different colors and sizes are strung on a store-bought belt—a neat way to organize things when you have to carry all kinds of small stuff.

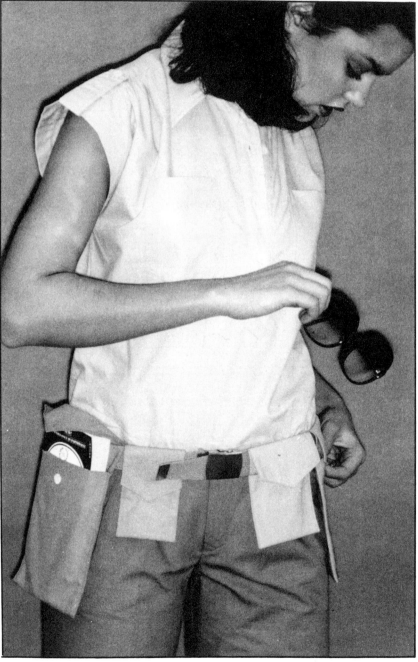

SIZE: Adjustable. Large pocket Is 6″ x 9″.

MATERIALS: 1½″-wide cotton web belt with metal buckle; hopsacking (or any cotton-type fabric), ¼ yard each in 4 colors; matching sewing thread; four ½″-diameter Velcro spot fasteners.

For largest pocket, cut one 7″ x 40″ piece of fabric. Fold in half crosswise and taper cut ends to point for flap. Unfold. Turn raw edges under ½″ and press.

With wrong sides together fold piece in half crosswise again, matching points, and baste outer edges together. To form flap, stitch across piece 1½″ from corners of tapered end (see broken line A on diagram), then continue topstitching around point from X to X.

To form belt casing, stitch across piece 1½″ below line A (see broken line B). Fold lower section up so that folded edge meets line B (see diagram). Pin edges and topstitch along sides to form pocket. Sew Velcro spots to dots. Insert belt through casing. Fold flap so that Velcro dots match.

Make 3 more pockets in same manner, the 1st from 5½″ x 37″ fabric, the 2nd from 5″ x 24″ fabric, and the 3rd from 4″ x 23″ fabric.

Construction Diagram for Pocket-packing Belt

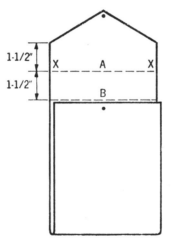

Pleated Circle Rug

This unusual and ingenious design consists of machine-pleated fabric strips—lightweight, closely woven cotton-blend fabrics in assorted prints and solids—that are sewn on unbleached muslin backing in overlapping rings.

SIZE: About 48" diameter.

MATERIALS: About 9 yards 45"-wide closely woven, light-weight, cotton-blend fabrics in assorted prints and solids; unbleached muslin large enough (pieced if necessary) to make 50" square for backing; matching sewing thread.

BACKING: Following diagram, fold muslin square in fourths. Cut 30" length of string; tie one end around a pencil and tape other end at folded corner of fabric, making sure that string span between corner and pencil is 25". Holding pencil so that string is taut, draw a quarter circle on fabric as shown. Cut out and unfold full circle. Turn edge under ¼", then turn under another ½" and topstitch, taking tiny tucks where necessary to make smooth edge.

With pencil, mark right side of backing from center out with concentric circles ¾" apart, starting with 1"-diameter circle at center.

TOP: Cut fabrics to be pleated (or ruffled) into 2½"-wide strips. Fold in half lengthwise and right side out; press.

Working with the appropriate attachment on your sewing machine, either pleat or gather raw edges of strips. (We pleated ours, making ¼"-deep pleats about ½" apart.)

Stitch strips to backing alternately from center and from outer edge, as follows: Cut a ruffled or gathered strip slightly longer than circumference of center circle. Lining up raw edges of strip to pencil line, overlap ends and topstitch in place, following pleating or gathering row of stitching and leaving center circle bare. Make a rosette from piece of stripping and sew to bare center.

Cut next strip to fit around outermost circle; stitch in place. Then cut another strip and stitch to next circle. Now go back to center and cut and stitch strips to fit around 2nd and 3rd circles from center. Complete rug in this manner, stitching 2 rows near outer edges, then 2 rows near center. Press on back every few rows to prevent puckering.

Construction Diagram for Pleated Circle Rug

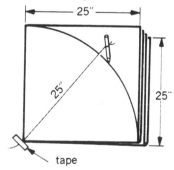

Patchwork Spread and Pillows

The cheery patchwork patterns here are variations on the old Log Cabin one. But these were given a new look by contrasting dark scraps with light ones for the Cherry Check and Blue-Green Cross pillows and the Red Square spread. The latter—which could also be a quilt or blanket cover—is diagonally striped with fabric blocks that repeat one color and pattern to make a dramatic design.

Construction Diagrams for Patchwork Spread and Pillows

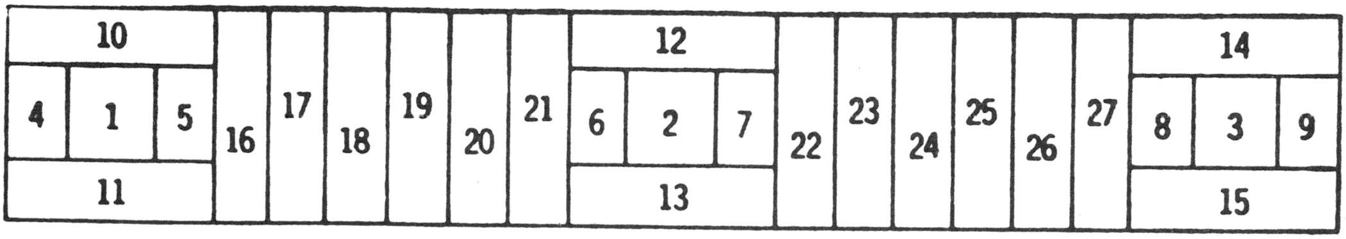

Blue-Green Cross Pillow   **First Band**

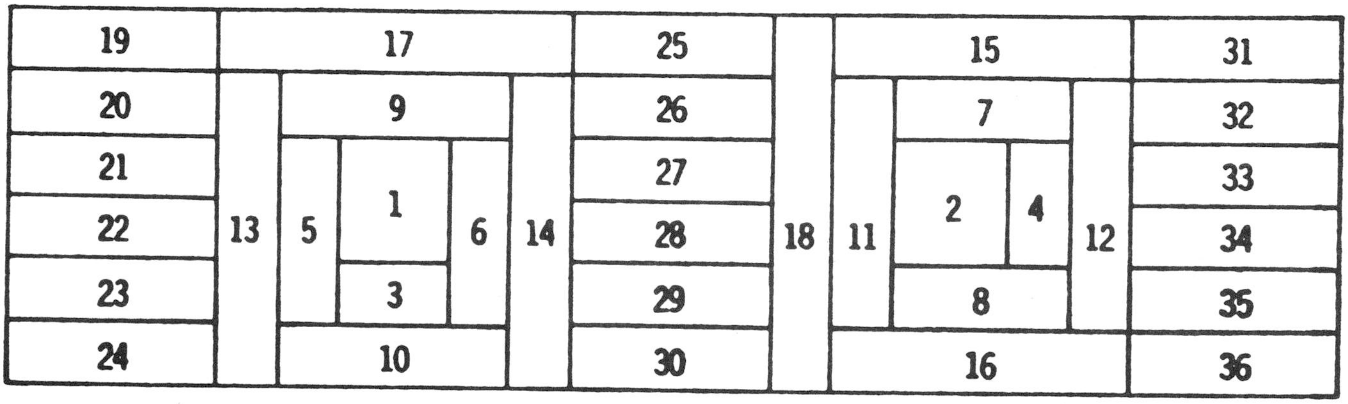

Cherry Check Pillow   **Second Band**

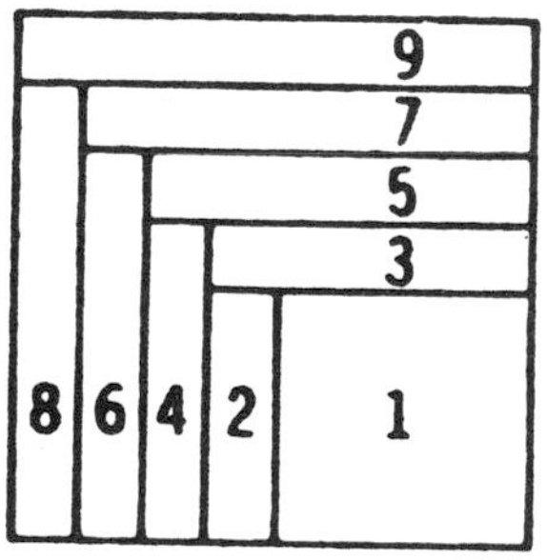

Square-Unit Diagram

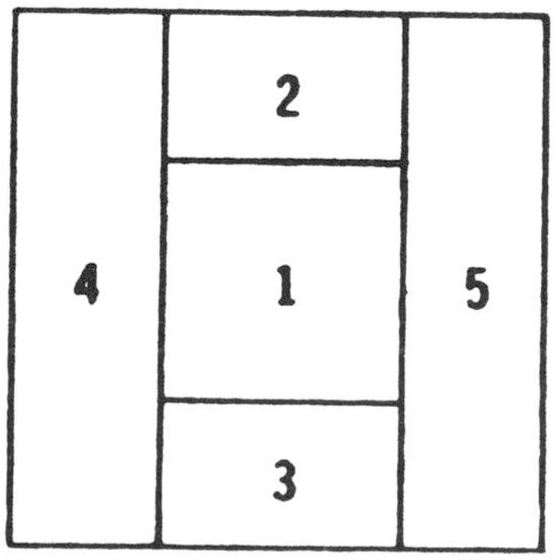

Band 1

strip

Spread
Square-Unit Diagram   **Spread-Diagram**

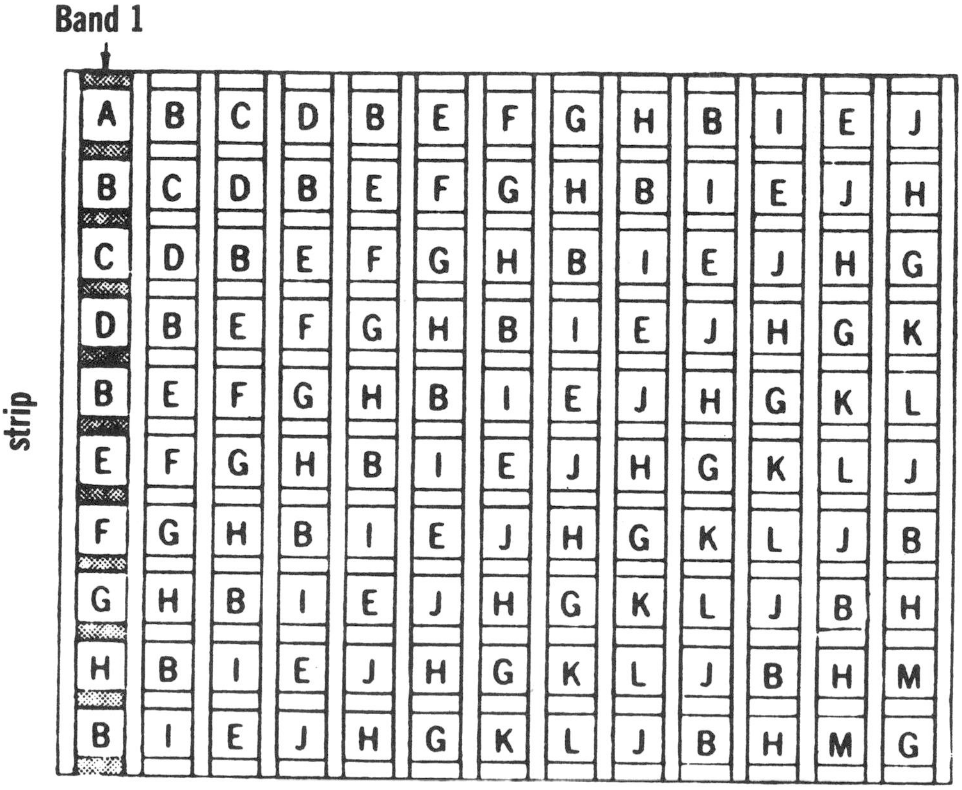

PATCHWORK SPREAD AND PILLOWS

GENERAL DIRECTIONS

Fabrics: Use closely woven, light- or medium-weight cotton fabrics in solid colors and prints. For each of the two pillows shown you will not need more than ¼ yard of any one color. The yardage for the spread is listed with the directions.

Cutting: Patterns for the patches are not necessary because all pieces are squares and rectangles and it is simple to cut them directly from the fabric, following dimensions we have given. *All dimensions include ½'' seam allowance.*

With pencil, ruler, and triangle draw the piece on wrong side of fabric, then draw stitching line ½'' in from outline.

Stitching: Hold two pieces to be joined, right sides facing and raw edges matching. Stitch along seam line and press all seams to one side.

RED SQUARE SPREAD

SIZE: About 6'5'' x 8'8''. Size is adjustable.

Color Note: The predominant color is red, with the same solid-red fabric used for all strips separating the square units. As can be seen in the photograph, each diagonal row of squares features a different print.

MATERIALS: You will need a piece of fabric about 8'' x 9'' for the predominant print in each square unit (2, 3, 4, and 5 on square-unit diagram). The center squares in units can be scraps. For strips separating the units you will need 4½ yards of 45''-wide fabric. For backing use one full-size sheet or 6 yards of 45''-wide fabric.

See General Directions.

SQUARE UNIT: Cut 1 square 3'' x 3'' (No. 1 on square-unit diagram). From one fabric cut 2 strips 2¾'' x 3'' (2 and 3 on diagram), and 2 strips 2¾'' x 6½'' (4 and 5).

Stitch strips 2 and 3 to opposite sides of square and strips 4 and 5 to remaining sides of square and to ends of strips 2 and 3. Make 129 more square units, following spread diagram for predominant color in each square: All A squares in one print, B squares in another print and so on. Size of spread can be adjusted by adding or omitting rows of units.

TO ASSEMBLE: From solid-color border fabric cut 11 strips

3'' x 6½''. Stitch them to 10 square units to form band 1 as shown on spread diagram. Shaded areas on band indicate strips. Make 12 more bands as shown. From same fabric cut 14 strips 3¼'' wide and as long as bands, piecing if necessary. Alternating them with bands, join to form spread.

BACKING: Cut and piece fabric or cut sheet to same size as spread. With right sides facing, stitch around 3½ sides. Turn and sew opening. Topstitch ½'' in from edge on all sides.

CHERRY CHECK PILLOW

SIZE: About 16'' x 20''.

Color Note: The predominant color is red, with the same solid-red fabric used for square (No. 1 on diagram) in each unit.

The pillow top is made by cutting squares and strips and joining them to form 20 square units that are then joined to form a rectangular pillow top. You can make your pillow top larger or smaller by making more or fewer units.

See General Directions.

SQUARE UNIT: Cut 1 square 3'' x 3'' (No. 1 on diagram). Cut 1 strip 1½'' x 3'' (2 on diagram), 2 strips 1½'' x 3½'' (3 and 4), 2 strips 1½'' x 4'' (5 and 6), 2 strips 1½'' x 4½ (7 and 8), and 1 strip 1½'' x 5'' (9).

Stitch strip 2 to 1, then strip 3 to 1 and to end of 2. Continue joining strips in sequence as shown to form square unit. Make 19 more units.

Join 5 units into a strip for length of pillow top. Make 3 more strips and join to form rectangle.

TO MAKE PILLOW: In addition to pieced top you will need a piece of cotton the same size as top for backing to complete cover. Use one of the fabrics from the pillow top, or you can make another pieced top in another color arrangement. You will also need 2 pieces of muslin for pillow lining the same size as top, and polyester-fiberfill stuffing. A zipper for one side of cover is optional.

Stitch muslin pieces together across 3 sides. Turn, stuff, and sew opening. With right sides facing, stitch pillow top and backing together across 3 sides. Add zipper if desired. Turn, insert pillow, and close zipper or blindstitch opening.

BLUE-GREEN CROSS PILLOW

SIZE: About 17" square.

Color Note: Blue and green predominate in this pillow. Strips numbered 4 through 15 on diagram for first band are all of same flowered print with black background.

The pillow top is made by cutting squares and strips and joining them to form 5 bands. The bands are then joined to form a square, and a ⅝" border is added to complete pillow top. You can make your pillow top larger or smaller by adjusting the length and number of bands.

See General Directions.

FIRST BAND: Cut 3 squares 2¼" x 2¼" (1, 2, and 3 on diagram for first band). Cut 6 strips 1⅝" x 2¼" (4 through 9) and 6 strips 1⅝" x 3½" (10 through 27).

Stitch strips 4 and 5 to two opposite sides of square 1. Stitch strips 10 and 11 to remaining two sides of square and to ends of strips 4 and 5. Stitch strip 16 to 5 and to ends of 10 and 11. Stitch strips 17 through 21 as shown. Then stitch strips 6, 7, 12, and 13 around square 2. Stitch this unit to strip 21. Complete band as shown. Make 2 more bands in same manner.

SECOND BAND: Cut 2 squares 2¼" x 2¼" (1 and 2 on diagram for 2nd band). Cut 2 strips 1⅝" x 2¼" (3 and 4), 4 strips 1⅝" x 2⅞" (5 through 8), 4 strips 1⅝" x 3½" (9 through 12), 4 strips 1⅝" x 4⅛" (13 through 16), 2 strips 1⅝" x 4¾" (17 and 18), and 18 strips 1⅝" x 3½" (19 through 36).

Stitch strip 3 to square 1, then 5 and 6 to opposite sides of square 1, and to ends of strip 3. Stitch strips 9 and 10 in place, then 13, 14, and 17 (unit 1 completed). Starting with square 2, make another unit in same manner. Stitch strips 19 through 24 together and join to side of unit 1. Continue joining strips and units to complete 2nd band as shown. Make another band in same manner.

Stitch first and second bands together alternately to form square. Cut 1⅝"-wide strips for border and sew in place.

TO MAKE PILLOW: See Cherry Check Pillow, page 157.

158